Animal Behavior and Mental Illness

Editor:
Undine E. Lang

Zeitschrift für Psychologie

Vol. 223, No. 3, 2015

HOGREFE

Library of Congress Cataloging in Publication

is available via the Library of Congress Marc Database under the
LC Control Number 2015950774

Cover image © jodie777 – fotolia.com

PUBLISHING OFFICES
USA: Hogrefe Publishing, 38 Chauncy Street, Suite 1002, Boston, MA 02111
Phone (866) 823-4726, Fax (617) 354-6875, E-mail customerservice@hogrefe.com
EUROPE: Hogrefe Publishing GmbH, Merkelstr. 3, 37085 Göttingen, Germany
Phone +49 551 99950-0, Fax +49 551 99950-425, E-mail publishing@hogrefe.com

SALES & DISTRIBUTION
USA: Hogrefe Publishing, Customer Services Department, 30 Amberwood Parkway, Ashland,
OH 44805, Phone (800) 228-3749, Fax (419) 281-6883, E-mail customerservice@hogrefe.com
UK: Hogrefe Publishing, c/o Marston Book Services Ltd., 160 Eastern Ave., Milton Park, Abingdon, OX14 4SB, UK
Phone +44 1235 465577, Fax +44 1235 465556; E-mail direct.orders@marston.co.uk
EUROPE: Hogrefe Publishing, Merkelstr. 3, 37085 Göttingen, Germany
Phone +49 551 99950-0, Fax +49 551 99950-425, E-mail publishing@hogrefe.com

OTHER OFFICES
CANADA: Hogrefe Publishing, 660 Eglinton Ave. East, Suite 119-514, Toronto, Ontario M4G 2K2
SWITZERLAND: Hogrefe Publishing, Länggass-Strasse 76, CH-3000 Bern 9

Hogrefe Publishing
Incorporated and registered in the Commonwealth of Massachusetts, USA, and in Göttingen, Lower Saxony, Germany

ISBN 978-0-88937-478-2

Contents

Editorial

What We Can Learn From Animal Behavior

Undine E. Lang

Department of Psychiatry and Psychotherapy, University Psychiatric Clinics (UPK), Basel, Switzerland

In this issue of the *Zeitschrift für Psychologie* we have assembled a number of articles and comments that deal with the role of animal behavior in neurobiological and psychological basic research, in behavioral models of psychiatric disorders, and in the treatment of psychiatric patients.

In a short review, Schweinfurth and Lang (2015) introduce several behavioral tests, which address symptoms of depression and anxiety and are commonly used in the development of new psychiatric drugs and the exploration of their efficacy.

Juckel (2015) describes how inflammational and immunological processes are connected with the pathophysiology of schizophrenia. In his article, he describes how microglia can induce a rarification of synaptic connections in frontal and temporal brain regions. In this context, he introduces promising inflammational animal models for schizophrenia with high validity that can be used to mimic behavioral as well as neurobiological findings in patients.

Two articles focus on new molecular pathways that might be highly relevant in the pathophysiology not only of cancer, viral infections, and obstetric complications, but also of affective disorders and schizophrenia. Phosphatidylinositol-3-kinase signaling has shown to be changed in patients with schizophrenia and their first degree relatives. In the article by Lang et al. (2015), a combined data set concerning human genetic, psychopathological, and electrophysiological, and animal neurotransmission data is shown. In conclusion, phosphatidylinositol-3-kinase signaling might have an impact on the pathophysiology of schizophrenia (Lang et al., 2015).

Additionally, the regulation of anxiety might be modulated by brain-derived neurotrophic dependent phosphatidylinositide-3-kinase signaling (Leibrock, Hierlmeier, Lang, & Lang, 2015). A behavioral study in mice shows differences in the behavior of gene targeted mice lacking functional Akt isoforms Akt1 (*akt1*$^{-/-}$) or Akt3 (*akt3*$^{-/-}$) when compared to that of wild type (*wt*) mice in the open-field test, light/dark transition test, O-maze test, and forced swimming test, which suggests them to be more anxious than their wild type controls (Leibrock et al., 2015).

In the article by Bolten (2015), the influence of early stress, maternal nutrition, social stress, and developmental influences is introduced and discussed.

In conclusion, this topical issue both reviews concepts, methodology, and application of behavioral animal test approaches to psychological research and carries them further by adding new facets. In addition, the influence of animals on human health is shown in a short Research Spotlight on an animal-assisted intervention for recurrent depression (Schramm, Hediger, & Lang, 2015). Several articles describe how animal behavioral tests can open new research directions and answer new molecular challenges. Furthermore, directions for future work are outlined and critically discussed.

References

Bolten, M. (2015). Transgenerational transmission of stress pathology: Contributions of rodent models. *Zeitschrift für Psychologie, 223*, 181–191. doi: 10.1027/2151-2604/a000219

Juckel, G. (2015). Inflammational animal models for schizophrenia. *Zeitschrift für Psychologie, 223*, 157–164. doi: 10.1027/2151-2604/a000216

Lang, U. E., Ackermann, T. F., Wolfer, D., Schubert, F., Sohr, R., Hörtnagl, H., . . ., & Gallinat, J. (2015). Phosphoinositide-dependent protein kinase 1 (PDK1): Impact on schizophrenia risk and endophenotype profil. *Zeitschrift für Psychologie, 223*, 165–172. doi: 10.1027/2151-2604/a000217

Leibrock, C., Hierlmeier, M., Lang, U. E., & Lang, F. (2015). Subtle impact of Akt1 and Akt3 on exploratory behavior in gene targeted mice. *Zeitschrift für Psychologie, 223*, 173–180. doi: 10.1027/2151-2604/a000218

Schramm, E., Hediger, K., & Lang, U. E. (2015). From animal behavior to human health: An animal-assisted mindfulness intervention for recurrent depression. *Zeitschrift für Psychologie, 223*, 192–200. doi: 10.1027/2151-2604/a000220

DOI: 10.1027/2151-2604/a000214

Schweinfurth, N., & Lang, U. E. (2015). Behavioural testing of mice concerning anxiety and depression: What can we learn from it? *Zeitschrift für Psychologie, 223*, 151–156. doi: 10.1027/2151-2604/a000215

Undine E. Lang

Department of Psychiatry and Psychotherapy
University Psychiatric Clinics (UPK)
Wilhelm Klein-Str. 27
4012 Basel
Switzerland
Tel. +41-325-5200
Fax +41-61-3255518
E-mail undine.lang@upkbs.ch

Review Article

Behavioral Testing of Mice Concerning Anxiety and Depression

What Can We Learn From it?

Nina Schweinfurth and Undine E. Lang

Department of Psychiatry, University Hospital of Basel (UPK), Switzerland

Abstract. In the development of new psychiatric drugs and the exploration of their efficacy, behavioral testing in mice has always shown to be an inevitable procedure. By studying the behavior of mice, diverse pathophysiological processes leading to depression, anxiety, and sickness behavior have been revealed. Moreover, laboratory research in animals increased at least the knowledge about the involvement of a multitude of genes in anxiety and depression. However, multiple new possibilities to study human behavior have been developed recently and improved and enable a direct acquisition of human epigenetic, imaging, and neurotransmission data on psychiatric pathologies. In human beings, the high influence of environmental and resilience factors gained scientific importance during the last years as the search for key genes in the development of affective and anxiety disorders has not been successful. However, environmental influences in human beings themselves might be better understood and controllable than in mice, where environmental influences might be as complex and subtle. The increasing possibilities in clinical research and the knowledge about the complexity of environmental influences and interferences in animal trials, which had been underestimated yet, question more and more to what extent findings from laboratory animal research translate to human conditions. However, new developments in behavioral testing of mice involve the animals' welfare and show that housing conditions of laboratory mice can be markedly improved without affecting the standardization of results.

Keywords: Anxiety, depression, animal models, behavioral testing, translational research

The reasons for exploring the molecular mechanisms of depression and anxiety are compelling. Both diseases occur in all genders, at all ages, and in all social backgrounds and in this context, they are the most common psychiatric disorders. Anxiety and depression are leading to immense costs, not only within the health system but also due to sickness-related absence or loss of productivity. Furthermore, depression and anxiety account in a tremendous way for an individual's disease burden which is reflected by disability adjusted live years (Mathers & Loncar, 2006). Increasing evidence also shows that both disorders constitute independent risk factors for the development of chronic medical conditions (Lang & Borgwardt, 2013).

In this context depression as such has been associated with the risk of developing cardiovascular disorders (Ramasubbu & Patten, 2003; Van der Kooy et al., 2007), stroke (Ramasubbu & Patten, 2003), Alzheimer's disease (Green et al., 2003), epilepsy (Hesdorffer, Hauser, Annegers, & Cascino, 2000), diabetes (Nouwen, Lloyd, & Pouwer, 2009), and cancer (Penninx et al., 1998). Also, anxiety states are more common in several medical conditions such as hypertension, diabetes, osteoporosis, and chronic obstructive pulmonary disease (COPD) (Bhattacharyha, Shen, & Sambamoorthi, 2014). Depression and anxiety co-occur in more than 50% of affected individuals (Bhattacharyha et al., 2014). Indeed, comorbid depression and anxiety are associated with several chronic physical conditions, that is, asthma, arthritis, back/neck problems, chronic headache, diabetes, cardiovascular disease, obesity, multiple pains, and ulcer (Scott et al., 2007). Vice versa all these disorders are expected to increase anxiety and depressive symptoms, which might challenge animal models, where sickness is usually measured.

Other challenges in research focus on depression and anxiety are the lack of any clear uniform neuropathological changes, monogenetic causes, or highly penetrating vulnerability genes. Also, both disorders represent a state (except phobia) rather than a trait reaction on multiple somatic and psychological situations. Moreover, specific human features of depression, which are a loss of interest, sadness, and loss of pleasure cannot be replicated/mimicked and/or observed appropriately in mice due to the inability to measure these feelings without language and scores. Several features that can be measured in animals, such as immobility, helplessness, anhedonia, phobic anxiety, and exploration are accessible but represent rather indirect symptoms, which can be influenced by multiple other conditions. Consequently, progress in understanding the molecular biology of depression has been extremely slow (Krishnan & Nestler, 2010).

Animal tests focus on the detection of a certain phenotypic trait and/or state. In contrast, animal models mimic a changed phenotype, which results in a depression-like behavior. Animal tests and models are not dispensable in the testing of psychotropic drugs, however the confidence

DOI: 10.1027/2151-2604/a000215

of researchers in animal models varies increasingly (Crabbe & Morris, 2004; Kalueff, Wheaton, & Murphy, 2007; Schmidt, 2011). Challenges of animal models are that there are features of human behavior, which cannot be reproduced in animal models, which are mostly selective simulations of a certain presumed pathology. One example is the knockout of one single gene in mutant mice. In human beings, however, genomewide association studies explained to us, that there is not one single genetic risk factor that will solely contribute to depressive pathology, which requires a genetic multifactorial vulnerability profile plus several environmental challenges. On the other hand, the often preferred focus on environmental stress, that is, adverse and stressful experiences neglects a genetic risk profile and/or resilience, which is highly variable in different individuals and enables human beings to adapt to adverse conditions (Charney, 2004). Therefore, the chance of detecting new compounds, new modes of action, and unsuspected results by using animal models has been questioned (Cryan, Mombereau, &, Vassout, 2005; Kalueff et al., 2007). Additionally, one problem might be that concerning psychiatric symptoms, the more standardized and thereby somehow artificial environmental conditions in mouse behavioral testing are, the less representative the results might be when translated to human conditions. For example, behavioral responses of animals might be disturbed (i.e., animals might be mentally disordered) when they are kept in small boxes, which is far from a physiological environment (Whishaw, Gharbawie, Clark, & Lehmann, 2006). In other words, concerns have been raised that an enriched environment might disrupt standardization, precision, and reproducibility of behavioral-tests in mutant mice. Indeed, reaching a physiological environment (with all implicated biological and psychological mechanisms of reaction of the individual) might distribute behavior and causes pathology only in a small amount of non-resilient animals.

Indeed, there is oversensitivity to external modulation in laboratory mice, where a high number of animals develop corresponding symptoms, due to an artificial environment with missing cues. In conclusion, tests are biased and the reproducibility varies highly (Cryan et al., 2005; Kalueff et al., 2007; Phillips et al., 2002; Schmidt, 2011; Wahlsten, Bachmanov, Finn, & Crabbe, 2006). However, new developments in behavioral testing of mice involve the animals' welfare, increase environmental enrichment, involve more physiological responses in psychologically less altered animals, and increase neither individual variability in behavioral tests nor the risk of obtaining conflicting data in replicate studies (Wolfer et al., 2004). Wolfer et al. show that housing conditions of laboratory mice can be markedly improved without affecting the standardization of results (Wolfer et al., 2004) and thereby establish more physiological conditions and increased psychological health in laboratory animals.

Montgomery was the first to assess anxiety, exploration, and fear in mice, which subsequently resulted in exploration tests, that is, the exploration in the open field, the development of novelty testing, emergence test, and the elevated plus maze (Montgomery, 1958). Common anxiety tests mimic specific phobic reactions, for example height anxiety.

In this context the *elevated x-maze* (Pellow & File, 1986) and the *elevated o-maze* (Handley & Mithani, 1984) have been developed. In the elevated o-maze for mice, an about 5 cm wide annular runway is constructed using gray polyvinyl chloride (PVC). It has an outer diameter of 46 cm and can be placed 40 cm above the floor (Lang et al., 2006; Leibrock et al., 2013). There are two opposing 90° closed sectors, which are protected by 11 cm high inner and outer walls of gray PVC, while the remaining two open sectors have a border of 5 mm. Animals are released in one of the closed sectors and are observed for 10 min (Figure 1). A 5.5 cm wide annular runway was constructed using white PVC. The two opposing 90° closed sectors were protected by 11 cm high inner and outer walls of white PVC, while the remaining two open sectors had a border of .5 cm. Animals were released in one of the closed sectors and observed for 10 min. A diagram illustrates the experimental setup in Figure 1.

In these tests open elevated arms are often avoided and mice are afraid of staying in open arms. Moreover, the number of head dips, that is looking in the depth, is an indicator of how fearful, courageous and/or curious an animal is. The *o-maze* and *x-maze* are tests to investigate anxiety-related behavior (Figure 1). The experiment assesses the urge of the mice to discover as well as their instinct to protect themselves. Mice usually avoid dangerous areas, but override their anxiety after a certain time because of curiosity. Important measures are, for example, if and how quickly they dare to leave the original protecting arm and enter the opposing area (Figure 1). If mice are treated with benzodiazepines they spend much more time in the open arms suggesting they are less fearful and are not retired in the projected environment. Multiple antidepressant drugs, such as imipramine (Teixeira, Zangrossi, & Graeff, 2000), clomipramine (Poltronieri, Zangrossi, & de Barros Viana, 2003), fluoxetine (Kõks et al., 2001), paroxetine (Griebel, Rodgers, Perrault, & Sanger, 1997), citalopram (Griebel et al., 1997), or mianserin (Griebel et al., 1997) are – as in phobic disorders- known to decrease anxiety (-related behavior) in the elevated plus maze and x-maze (Figure 1).

The *light-dark box* was introduced by Crawley et al. (Crawley & Goodwin, 1980) (Figure 2). This test deals with the fear of rodents for illuminated bright, open, and therefore unprotected places. This might be comparable with the phobic anxiety of human beings with agoraphobia, where large, visible, and unsafe places are avoided to be able to escape from possible predators and followers. The light-dark box is based on the fact that mice avoid bright light but at the same time want to explore the unknown environment (Figure 2). The light-dark box creates a conflict for the mouse that tends to explore the unfamiliar area and initially wants to avoid the unfamiliar area. In a 5–10 min session, the mice are allowed to freely explore a dark, protected house or an unprotected illuminated exposed zone. The main outcome parameters measured in the light-dark box are the latency time to enter the light compartment from the dark one, the number of transitions

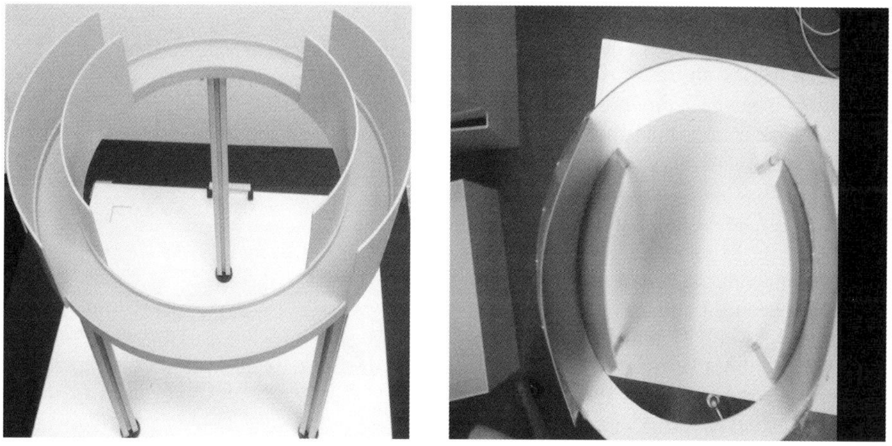

Figure 1. Elevated o-maze. The o-maze test investigates anxiety-related behavior. The pictures (on the left: view from above; on the right: bird's eye view) show a typical test set-up with an about 5 cm wide annular polyvinyl chloride (PVC) runway with an outer diameter of 46 cm, placed 40 cm above the floor. The two opposing 90° closed sectors are protected by 11 cm high inner and outer PVC walls. The two open sectors have a border of 0.5 cm. Animals are being released in one of the closed sectors and are observed for 10 min. During this period, for example, time spent in the closed versus open sectors, or number of head dips are assessed. Pictures courtesy of Undine E. Lang.

between the light and dark compartment, the movement in each compartment, and the time spent in each of them, rearing and grooming as a sort of well-feeling behavior are also recorded (Figure 2). If animals are treated with different anxiolytic drugs the time spent in the bright unprotected zone will increase and the number of transitions between the two compartments will also increase. Normally, the apparatus of the light-dark box for mice consists of an infrared permeable box made of black acryl (40 cm high), which is inserted into the open-field arena and covers 33% of the surface area. An aperture of 10 cm length and 11 cm height with rounded down corners lets light from the arena to the dark box. Each subject is released in the corner of the lit compartment and is observed for 5–10 min. The experiment is performed under direct room light (Crawley & Goodwin, 1980) (Figure 2).

Figure 2. Light-dark box. The light-dark box is another test to investigate anxiety-related behavior in rodents. As depicted in Figure 2 the test set-up consists of an infrared permeable box of 40 cm of height made of black acryl, which is inserted into an open-field arena and covers 33% of the surface area. An aperture of 10 cm length and 11 cm height with rounded down corners lets from the light arena into the dark box. The experiment is performed under direct room light. Each subject is released in the corner of the lit compartment and observed for 5–10 min, where it can freely explore the set-up. During the observation period, the following measures can be assessed: (1) latency time to enter the light compartment from the dark one, (2) number of transitions between the light and dark compartment, (3) movement in each compartment and the time spent in each of them, (4) rearing and grooming behavior. Picture courtesy of Undine E. Lang.

Immobility

Restraint stress and immobilization protocols are one of the most widely employed procedures to examine the behavioral, biological, and biochemical basis of stress-induced behavior (Campos, Fogaca, Aguiar, & Guimaraes, 2013). Restraint stress is generally introduced by keeping the animals in a cylindrical tube with ventilation holes for 120–180 min (Padovan & Guimaraes, 2000). The forced swim test was introduced by Porsolt (2000), who showed that despair can be used to assess the effects of antidepressant drugs (Porsolt, 2000). The forced swim and tail suspension tests are the simplest and most widely utilized models of depression and antidepressant action (Krishnan & Nestler, 2010). However, these approaches are highly stressful for the animal, involve acute vital fear responses, and have been criticized for the involvement of acute traumatic stress responses. However, forced swim test and tail suspension test are highly sensitive in testing the behavioral changes after treatment with novel chemical antidepressants, show fast and reliable results concerning the phenotyping of genetically altered mutant mice, and are very easy to establish and perform. In certain instances, they have directed the field toward fundamentally novel molecular hypotheses (Krishnan & Nestler, 2010).

In the *forced swim test* mice are placed in a container of water with temperatures between 24 and 26 °C. The diameter of the container ranges between 15 and 25 cm and the mouse is placed in the water without being able to touch the ground. Mice are observed for 6 min and the time they spent without movement, called floating, is recorded. It has been shown and robustly replicated that the time of immobility is reduced by antidepressants (Porsolt, 2000; Porsolt, Le Pichon, & Jalfre, 1977; Prickaerts et al., 2006). Thus, differences between genotypes may allow conclusions about their depressive behavior.

The *tail suspension test* was invented by Steru, Chermat, Thierry, and Simon (1985). Similar to the forced swim test, in the tail suspension test mice are placed in an inescapable but moderately stressful situation (Can et al., 2012). The tail suspension test is validated as an experimental procedure to assess antidepressant efficacy of drug treatments in mice (Can et al., 2012). Mice are suspended by their tails with tape in a situation where they cannot escape for 6 min and their escape activities are recorded and quantified (Can et al., 2012). Lack of escape-related behavior is considered immobility. Like the forced swim test, the tail suspension test is a test best validated for the evaluation of antidepressant efficacy of drugs, but also used to evaluate the effects of environmental, neurobiological and genetic manipulations (Can et al., 2012).

Learned helplessness models are based on the impact of the uncontrollability of events on the emotional state of an individual (Maier, 1984). Indeed, the degree to which organisms can exert control over events to which they are exposed has a strong impact on their behavior, emotions, and physiological functioning (Maier, 1984).

The concept of learned helplessness defines an escape or avoidance deficit after uncontrollable stress and is regarded as a depression-like coping deficit in aversive but avoidable situations (Vollmayr & Gass, 2013).

The *open-field test* was introduced by Hall (1934) and is a method to analyze locomotor and mood-related behavior. Besides speed and total distance moved that give information about the general activity of mice, it is a matter of particular interest as to which zone of the open field the mice prefer. Anxious behavior is reflected by staying in the corners and the border area, whereas audacious behavior is indicated by exploration of the center of the arena. The quadratic arena has side lengths of 50 cm, a white plastic floor, and 40 cm high sidewalls. Each subject is released near the wall and observed for 30 min (Madani et al., 2003). For evaluation, a border with 10 cm distance to the wall is considered. The quadratic arena has side lengths of 50 cm, a white plastic floor and 40 cm high sidewalls. Each subject is released near the wall and observed for 30 min.

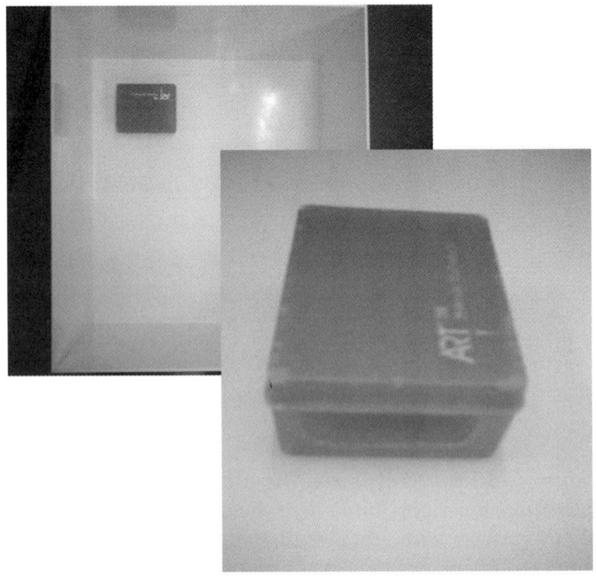

Figure 3. Emergence test. The emergence test assesses the anxious component of responses to approach-avoidance conflicts. The test was designed to reduce anxiety by providing a safe enclosure within the open-field. Figure 3 shows in the upper picture an infra-red permeable box, which first is placed in the home cage of the mouse for more than 24 hrs. The home box has a base area of 9 × 10 cm with two apertures of 3 cm of length and 3.5 cm of height with rounded down corners on the long sides. Then the box is placed in an arena (open-field; Figure 3 lower picture) and the mouse is observed for 30 min. The following measures can be assessed: (1) time spent in or near the familiar home box, (2) over all locomotor activity. Picture courtesy of Undine E. Lang.

For evaluation, a border with 10 cm distance to the wall is considered.

The following describes a modified version of the *emergence test* proposed by Dulawa, Grandy, Low, Paulus, and Geyer (1999). An infra red permeable box, which is in a first step placed in the home cage of the mouse for more than 24 hrs, is inserted into the arena (Figure 3). The home box has a base area of 9 × 10 cm with two apertures (3 cm length, 3.5 cm height with rounded down corners) on the long sides (Figure 3). The mouse is observed for 30 min. This test examines the behavior of mice in an area during the presence of a familiar object. The main interest is the time spent in or near the familiar home box (Figure 3).

The following illustrates a modified version of the *object exploration test* also proposed by Dulawa et al. (1999). The arena is usually the same as for the open field and the emergence test. The mouse is first observed for 30 min in the open-field arena including the home box. Afterwards, a Falcon® tube is additionally put into the arena and fixed with adhesive tape (Figure 4). The mouse is then observed for another 30 min and the contact with the nose on the falcon tube is taken as criterion to analyze the reaction on the novel object.

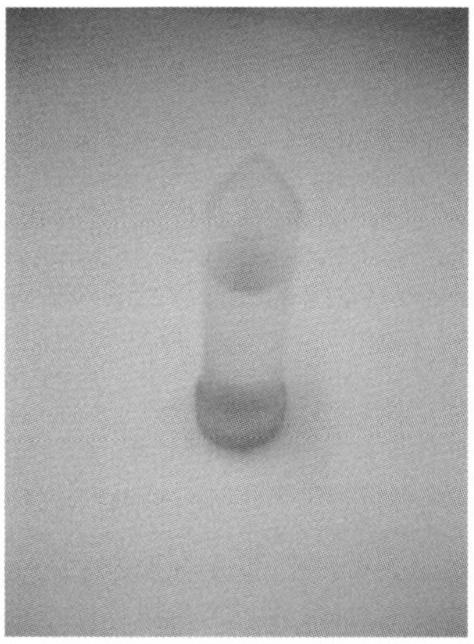

Figure 4. Object exploration test. Similar to the emergence test, the object exploration test investigates responses to approach-avoidance conflicts. The first part of the test consists of the same (pre-)set-up as in the emergence test, where the mouse is observed in an open-field where a familiar object (home box) is placed. For the object exploration test, as a new object, a Falcon® tube is placed additionally in the open-field arena and fixed with adhesive tape (Figure 4). During a period of another 30 min the following measures can be assessed: (1) mouse's nose dips to new object, (2) locomotor activity, (3) time spent in different parts of the field (e.g. near familiar object vs. near new object). Picture courtesy of Undine E. Lang.

Indeed, impaired brain development, stereotypies, and an anxious behavioral profile are displayed by mice when housed in standard laboratory cages (Wolfer et al., 2004). Poor reliability and low efficiency of traditional behavioral tests have prompted the development of new approaches to behavioral phenotyping, such as fully automated analysis of behavior in the social home cage (Vannoni et al., 2014). Thereby, it has been shown that the enrichment of cages does not decrease the sensitivity of tests for detecting genetic differences, that is, it is applicable and shows advantages for the mice and improves the examined animals' well-being (Wolfer et al., 2004).

Conclusion

Currently, there are multiple behavioral testings next to different animal models available, sought to measuring anxiety- and depressive-like behavior, for example in wild-type and/or mutant rodents. The terminology *animal models* and *behavioral testing* needs careful differentiation within the scientific community, that is, in *animal models*, a particular pathology is evoked and in *animal testing* specific responses to controlled situations are measured. Animal tests are invaluable tools for a first *in vivo* model assessment of pharmacological interventions addressing new therapeutic targets, or for demonstrating whether a certain genotype translates to altered behavioral features. However, facing the uncertainties related to (non-) genetic risk factors, pathophysiology, and even the nosology of most human psychiatric disorders, in line with a lack of objective medical tests or availability of biomarkers for these disease entities, a direct translation from animal research results to human (disease) conditions should be considered critically. In the near future advances in human beings centered research involving and combining a plethora of methodological approaches ranging from molecular techniques to neuroimaging and clinical outcome parameters should help redefine and optimize current animal (disease) models and testing paradigms, as well as generate new model systems facilitating to elucidate the complex (molecular) underpinnings in human disease with better validity.

References

Bhattacharyha, R., Shen, C., & Sambamoorthi, U. (2014). Excess risk of chronic physical conditions associated with depression and anxiety. *Biomedcentral Psychiatry, 14*, 10.

Campos, A. C., Fogaca, M. V., Aguiar, D. C., & Guimaraes, F. S. (2013). Animal models of anxiety disorders and stress. *Revista Brasileira de Psiquiatria, 35*, S101–S111.

Can, A., Dao, D. T., Terrillion, C. E., Piantadosi, S. C., Bhat, S., & Gould, T. D. (2012). The tail suspension test. *Journal of Visualized Experiments, 59*, 3769.

Charney, D. S. (2004). Psychobiological mechanisms of resilience and vulnerability: Implications for successful adaptation to extreme stress. *The American Journal of Psychiatry, 161*, 195–216.

Crabbe, J. C., & Morris, R. G. (2004). Festina lente: Late-night thoughts on high-throughput screening of mouse behavior. *Nature Neuroscience, 7*, 1175–1179.

Crawley, J., & Goodwin, F. K. (1980). Preliminary report of a simple animal behavior model for the anxiolytic effects of benzodiazepines. *Pharmacology Biochemistry and Behavior, 13*, 167–170.

Cryan, J. F., Mombereau, C., & Vassout, A. (2005). The tail suspension test as a model for assessing antidepressant activity: Review of pharmacological and genetic studies in mice. *Neuroscience & Biobehavioral Reviews, 29*, 571–625.

Dulawa, S. C., Grandy, D. K., Low, M. J., Paulus, M. P., & Geyer, M. A. (1999). Dopamine D4 receptor-knock-out mice exhibit reduced exploration of novel stimuli. *The Journal of Neuroscience, 19*, 9550–9556.

Green, R. C., Cupples, L. A., Kurz, A., Auerbach, S., Go, R., Sadovnick, D., . . . Farrer, L. (2003). Depression as a risk factor for Alzheimer disease: The MIRAGE study. *Archives of Neurology, 60*, 753–759.

Griebel, G., Rodgers, R. J., Perrault, G., & Sanger, D. J. (1997). Risk assessment behaviour: Evaluation of utility in the study of 5-HT-related drugs in the rat elevated plus-maze test. *Pharmacology Biochemistry and Behavior, 57*, 817–827.

Hall, C. S. (1934). Emotional behavior of the rat. Defecation and urination as measures of the individual differences in emotionality. *Journal of Comparative Psychology, 18*, 385–403.

Handley, S. L., & Mithani, S. (1984). Effects of alpha-adrenoceptor agonists and antagonists in a maze-exploration model of "fear"-motivated behaviour. *Naunyn Schmiedebergs Archives of Pharmacology, 327*, 1–5.

Hesdorffer, D. C., Hauser, W. A., Annegers, J. F., & Cascino, G. (2000). Major depression is a risk factor for seizures in older adults. *Annals of Neurology, 47*, 246–249.

Kalueff, A. V., Wheaton, M., & Murphy, D. L. (2007). What's wrong with my mouse model? Advances and strategies in animal modeling of anxiety and depression. *Behavioural Brain Research, 179*, 1–18.

Kõks, S., Beljajev, S., Koovit, I., Abramov, U., Bourin, M., & Vasar, E. (2001). 8-OH-DPAT, but not deramciclane, antagonizes the anxiogenic-like action of paroxetine in an elevated plus-maze. *Psychopharmacology (Berl), 153*, 365–372.

Krishnan, V., & Nestler, E. J. (2010). Linking molecules to mood: New insight into the biology of depression. *The American Journal of Psychiatry, 167*, 1305–1320.

Lang, U. E., & Borgwardt, S. (2013). Molecular mechanisms of depression: Perspectives on new treatment strategies. *Cellular Physiology and Biochemistry, 31*, 761–777.

Lang, U. E., Wolfer, D. P., Grahammer, F., Strutz-Seebohm, N., Seebohm, G., Lipp, H. P., Dawson, K., … Lang, F. (2006). Reduced locomotion in the serum and glucocorticoid inducible kinase 3 knock out mouse. *Behavioural Brain Research, 167*, 75–86.

Leibrock, C., Ackermann, T. F., Hierlmeier, M., Lang, F., Borgwardt, S., & Lang, U. E. (2013). Akt2 deficiency is associated with anxiety and depressive behaviour in mice. *Cellular Physiology and Biochemistry, 32*, 766–777.

Madani, R., Kozlov, S., Akhmedov, A., Cinelli, P., Kinter, J., Lipp, H. P., … Wolfer, D. P. (2003). Impaired explorative behavior and neophobia in genetically modified mice lacking or overexpressing the extracellular serine protease inhibitor neuroserpin. *Molecular and Cellular Neuroscience, 23*, 473–494.

Maier, S. F. (1984). Learned helplessness and animal models of depression. *Progress in Neuro-Psychopharmacology and Biological Psychiatry, 8*, 435–446.

Mathers, C. D., & Loncar, D. (2006). Projections of global mortality and burden of disease from 2002 to 2030. *PLoS Med, 3*(11), e442.

Montgomery, K. C. (1958). The relation between fear induced by novel stimulation and exploratory behaviour. *Journal of Comparative and Physiological Psychology, 48*, 254–260.

Nouwen, A., Lloyd, C. E., & Pouwer, F. (2009). Depression and type 2 diabetes over the lifespan: A meta-analysis. *Response to Mezuk et al. Diabetes Care, 32*, 56–57.

Padovan, C. M., & Guimaraes, F. S. (2000). Restraint-induced hypoactivity in an elevated plus-maze. *Brazilian Journal of Medical and Biological Research, 33*, 79–83.

Pellow, S., & File, S. E. (1986). Anxiolytic and anxiogenic drug effects on exploratory activity in an elevated plus-maze: A novel test of anxiety in the rat. *Pharmacology Biochemistry and Behavior, 24*, 525–529.

Penninx, B. W., Guralnik, J. M., Pahor, M., Ferrucci, L., Cerhan, J. R., Wallace, R. B., & Havlik, R. J. (1998). Chronically depressed mood and cancer risk in older persons. *Journal of the National Cancer Institute, 90*, 1888–1893.

Phillips, T. J., Belknap, J. K., Hitzemann, R. J., Buck, K. J., Cunningham, C. L., & Crabbe, J. C. (2002). Harnessing the mouse to unravel the genetics of human disease. *Genes, Brain and Behavior, 1*, 14–26.

Poltronieri, S. C., Zangrossi, H. Jr., & de Barros Viana, M. (2003). Antipanic-like effect of serotonin reuptake inhibitors in the elevated T-maze. *Behavioural Brain Research, 147*, 185–192.

Porsolt, R. D. (2000). Animal models of depression: Utility for transgenic research. *Reviews Neuroscience, 11*, 53–58.

Porsolt, R. D., Le Pichon, M., & Jalfre, M. (1977). Depression: A new animal model sensitive to antidepressant treatments. *Nature, 266*, 730–732.

Prickaerts, J., Moechars, D., Cryns, K., Lenaerts, I., van Craenendonck, H., Goris, I., … Steckler, T. (2006). Transgenic mice overexpressing glycogen synthase kinase 3beta: A putative model of hyperactivity and mania. *The Journal of Neuroscience, 26*, 9022–9029.

Ramasubbu, R., & Patten, S. B. (2003). Effect of depression on stroke morbidity and mortality. *Canadian Journal of Psychiatry, 48*, 250–257.

Schmidt, M. V. (2011). Animal models for depression and the mismatch hypothesis of disease. *Psychoneuroendocrinology, 36*, 330–338.

Scott, K. M., Bruffaerts, R., Tsang, A., Ormel, J., Alonso, J., Angermeyer, M. C., … Von Korff, M. (2007). Depression-anxiety relationships with chronic physical conditions: Results from the World Mental Health Surveys. *Journal of Affective Disorders, 103*, 113–120.

Steru, L., Chermat, R., Thierry, B., & Simon, P. (1985). The tail suspension test: A new method for screening antidepressants in mice. *Psychopharmacology (Berl), 85*, 367–370.

Teixeira, R. C., Zangrossi, H., & Graeff, F. G. (2000). Behavioral effects of acute and chronic imipramine in the elevated T-maze model of anxiety. *Pharmacology Biochemistry and Behavior, 65*, 571–576.

Van der Kooy, K., van Hout, H., Marwijk, H., Marten, H., Stehouwer, C., & Beekman, A. (2007). Depression and the risk for cardiovascular diseases: Systematic review and meta-analysis. *International Journal of Geriatric Psychiatry, 22*, 613–626.

Vannoni, E., Voikar, V., Colacicco, G., Sánchez, M. A., Lipp, H. P., & Wolfer, D. P. (2014). Spontaneous behavior in the social homecage discriminates strains, lesions and mutations in mice. *Journal of Neuroscience Methods, 234*, 26–37.

Vollmayr, B., & Gass, P. (2013). Learned helplessness: Unique features and translational value of a cognitive depression model. *Cell and Tissue Research, 354*, 171–178.

Wahlsten, D., Bachmanov, A., Finn, D. A., & Crabbe, J. C. (2006). Stability of inbred mouse strain differences in behavior and brain size between laboratories and across decades. *Proceedings of the National Academy of Sciences of the United States of America, 103*, 16364–16369.

Whishaw, I. Q., Gharbawie, O. A., Clark, B. J., & Lehmann, H. (2006). The exploratory behavior of rats in an open environment optimizes security. *Behavioural Brain Research, 171*, 230–239.

Wolfer, D. P., Litvin, O., Morf, S., Nitsch, R. M., Lipp, H. P., & Würbel, H. (2004). Laboratory animal welfare: Cage enrichment and mouse behaviour. *Nature, 432*, 821–822.

Undine E. Lang

Department of Psychiatry
University Psychiatric Clinics (UPK)
Wilhelm Klein-Str. 27
4012 Basel
Switzerland
Tel. +41-325-5200
Fax +41-61-3255518
E-mail undine.lang@upkbs.ch

Original Article

Inflammational Animal Models for Schizophrenia

Georg Juckel

Department of Psychiatry, Ruhr University, LWL University Hospital, Bochum, Germany

Abstract. Inflammational-immunological processes within the pathophysiology of schizophrenia seem to play an important role. Early signals of neurobiological changes in the embryonal phase of brain in later patients with schizophrenia might lead to activation of the immunological system, for example, of cytokines and microglial cells. Microglia then induces – via the neurotoxic activities of these cells as an overreaction – a rarification of synaptic connections in frontal and temporal brain regions, that is, reduction of the neuropil. Promising inflammational animal models for schizophrenia with high validity can be used today to mimic behavioral as well as neurobiological findings in patients, for example, the well-known neurochemical alterations of dopaminergic, glutamatergic, serotonergic, and other neurotransmitter systems. Also the microglial activation can be modeled well within one of this models, that is, the inflammational PolyI:C animal model of schizophrenia, showing a time peak in late adolescence/early adulthood. The exact mechanism, by which activated microglia cells then triggers further neurodegeneration, must now be investigated in broader detail. Thus, these animal models can be used to understand the pathophysiology of schizophrenia better especially concerning the interaction of immune activation, inflammation, and neurodegeneration. This could also lead to the development of anti-inflammational treatment options and of preventive interventions.

Keywords: inflammational animal models, schizophrenia, dopamine, glutamate, microglia, neurodegeneration

The so-called "neurodevelopmental hypothesis" is a leading hypothesis today about the pathophysiology of schizophrenia. Impairment of important brain developmental genes in the 2. trimenon of pregnancy leads to disturbances of the normal brain maturation with the result of neurotransmitter imbalance and dysfunction of the limbic system, accompanied by structural changes in the areas of hippocampus, regio entorhinalis, and the ventricular system (Falkai et al., 2003; Heinz et al., 1999; Juckel et al., 1994, Juckel, Sass, & Heinz, 2003; Juckel, Müller-Schubert, Gaebel, & Hegerl, 1996; Weinberger, 1995). This neural dysgenesis becomes clinically relevant with considerable postnatal delay. It is supposed that further brain development processes or additional pathogenic factors are likely to elicit the illness finally (Heinz, Romero, Gallinat, Juckel, & Weinberger, 2003; Heinz & Weinberger, 2000). In many patients, progressive cortical volume reduction is found mainly in frontotemporal regions (gyrus cinguli, prefrontal cortex) (Cahn et al., 2002; Mathalon, Sullivan, Lim, & Pfefferbaum, 2001; Pantelis et al., 2003). These findings may be caused by a reduction of neuropil with relatively increased number of cells (Scherk, Vogeley, & Falkai, 2003).

Inflammational and immunological reactions are discussed as being main reasons for the impairment of brain development in the 2. trimenon. Big cohort studies have shown the result, that children of mothers who suffered from, for example, influenza in the 2. trimenon, developed schizophrenic disorders more often than others (Limosin, Rouillon, Payan, Cohen, & Strub, 2003; Mednick, Machon, Huttunen, & Bonett, 1988; Munk-Jørgensen & Ewald, 2001; Takei, Lewis, Jones, Harvey, & Murray, 1996). Serologic evidence also points to multiple prenatal exposures to various viruses as causative factors in rise of schizophrenic births with a 7-fold increase of risk (Brown et al., 2004). This could be the reason for the activation of the immune system and immune competent cells in schizophrenia, which was often found in patients with schizophrenic disorders for years. Thus, the unspecific immune system shows clear signs of overactivation in unmedicated patients with schizophrenic disorders with an increased number of gamma/delta cells and monocytes/macrophages, and, as a consequence of the activation of these cells, an increase of interleukin 6 (Gaughran, 2002; Müller et al., 1997, 1998). The specific immune system shows an imbalance of cytokines in favor of an increased activity of T-helper cells; in addition, there were changes in the immunglobulins, antibodies, and the complement system (Müller & Ackenheil, 1998; Rothermundt, Arolt, & Bayer, 2001). Interestingly, a 5-week add-on therapy with the anti-inflammational substance celecoxib, a COX-2 inhibitor, showed better clinical improvement in acute patients with schizophrenic disorders than the treatment with the atypical neuroleptic risperidone alone (Müller et al., 2002).

Activation of microglia/macrophages is a key event in the reaction of the central neuro-immune system as an answer to any pathological changes (Kreutzberg, 1996; Monji, Kato, & Kanba, 2009). Two postmortem studies found activated microglia (stained by HLA-DR) in older patients with chronic schizophrenic disorders in particular in the dorsolateral prefrontal cortex (DLPFC), in the gyrus

DOI: 10.1027/2151-2604/a000216

temporalis superior (GTS), and in the anterior gyrus cinguli (ACC), which are known as the main areas of schizophrenic pathophysiology (Bayer, Buslei, Havas, & Falkai, 1999; Radewicz, Garey, Gentleman, & Reynolds, 2000). Concerning astroglia, no differences were found in these two first studies. Activated microglia could either be a reaction of the brain immune system to a constant disturbance of neuroplasticity due to, for example, the degenerative changes that are found in the patient suffering from schizophrenia (increasing number of microglia cells with age) or could be stored as an early answer to any inflammatory or noninflammatory events during pregnancy staying up to the adult age (relatively stable cell number) (Munn, 2000; Radewicz et al., 2000; Rothermundt et al., 2001). Thus, activated microglia could lead to neuropil reduction with rarification of synapses, dendrites, and spines in patients with schizophrenic disorders due to their neurotoxic properties (e.g., release of cytokines or free radicals), either in the early stage of brain development or progressively with the course of illness (Radewicz et al., 2000). Many questions on the role of activated microglia for schizophrenia are still unexplained. Furthermore, there is still no proof of activated microglia in vivo in patients suffering from schizophrenia. Using PK11195, a PET ligand for the peripheral benzodiazepine receptor, which is expressed in activated microglia, the Dutch working group around R. Kahn was able to find first hints that there seem to be more activated microglial cells in living patients with schizophrenia (van Berckel et al., 2008), which was replicated by Doorduin et al. (2009).

A promising animal model of the inflammatory genesis of schizophrenia is the model of the motherly influenza infection in mice (BALB/c) developed by Hossein Fatemi in Minneapolis (Fatemi, Earle, et al., 2002; Fatemi, Halt, et al., 2002; Fatemi, Sidwell, Akhter, et al., 1998; Fatemi, Sidwell, Kist, et al., 1998; Fatemi et al., 1999, 2000; Shi, Fatemi, Sidwell, & Patterson, 2003). Descendants of female mice, who were exposed to a mouse-adapted influenza virus in the middle of pregnancy and had gone through a respiratory infection, show several changes in brain morphology, physiology, and behavior after puberty (fertility) comparably to those of schizophrenic patients. Influenza infection at E9 of pregnancy in mice leads to abnormal corticogenesis, pyramidal cell atrophy, and alterations in levels of several neuroregulatory proteins, such as reelin, and GFAP, in the exposed mouse progeny: volume reduction of neocortex and hippocampus with relatively raised cell number, pyramid cell dystrophy, wide ventricles, reduced reelin and immune reactivity, changes from nNOS and SNAP-25, deficits in prepulse inhibition (PPI) within the acoustic startle response, in the open field test, in the novel object test, and in social interactions (Fatemi et al., 1999; Fatemi, Earle, et al., 2002; Fatemi, Halt, et al., 2002; Shi et al., 2003; see Table 1).

A further promising animal model is the administration of viral mimetic polyriboinosinic-polyribocytidilic acid (PolyI:C) in vulnerable periods during pregnancy: Descendants of female mice, who were exposed to PolyI:C at day 9, show changes in brain morphology, physiology, and chemistry as well as in behavior after puberty that are partly reminiscent of changes observed in human schizophrenia (e.g., Meyer & Feldon, 2010; e.g., Winter et al., 2009). Especially, the following findings were described (Meyer, 2014):

- Impairments in several behavioral measurements including PPI, LI, startle response, sensory gating, etc.
- Changes in interleukin-10 and -1 beta, and other immune reactions.
- Changes in GABA-A receptors in limbic areas.
- Dopamine- and glutamate-related pharmacological and neuroanatomical disturbances.
- Reduced D1 receptors in PFC and reduced hippocampal NMDA receptor.
- Increased number of mesencephalic dopamine neurons in the fetal brain (middle/late gestation) (accompanied by specific gene changes).
- Reduction of reelin- and parvalbumin expressing PFC neurons.

Evidence has shown that the time of prenatal insult may provide distinct changes in the exposed offspring. In a recent series of experiments by Meyer et al. (2006) using the viral mimic polyribocytidilic acid (PolyI:C) at E9 (which corresponds to midpregnancy) and E17 (which corresponds to late pregnancy), there were distinct behavioral deficits, neuropathological differences, and acute cytokine responses (Meyer et al., 2006). Adult mice that were exposed on E9 displayed reduced exploratory behavior while those exposed on E17 displayed perseverative behavior (Meyer et al., 2006). At P24, mice that were exposed on E9 displayed a more pronounced reduction of reelin immunoreactivity in hippocampus than mice exposed at E17 (Meyer et al., 2006). In contrast, mice exposed at E17 displayed an increase in apoptosis as visualized by immunoreactivity of caspase-3, a key enzyme involved in apoptosis (Rami, 2003), in the dorsal dentate gyrus (Meyer et al., 2006). Finally, Meyer et al. (2006) found that late gestational immune challenge uniquely stimulated increased IL-10 and TNF-α in fetal brain (Meyer et al., 2006). Taken together, these results provide evidence that the time of prenatal insult results in important differences that are persistent through adulthood.

Table 1. Similar chances of behavioral and neurobiological markers in influenza mouse model and in patients with schizophrenia (adapted from Fatemi)

Group	Brain markers			Brain structure		Brain genes				Behavior
Influenza mouse model	nNOS	Reelin	GFAP	Pyramidal cell atrophy	Brain atrophy	MBP	PLP	Net-nd P	HSCP70	Prepulse inhibition
Adulthood schizophrenia	↓	↓	↑	+	+	↓	↓	↑	↑	Abnormal
Adulthood	↓	↓	↓/–	+	+	↓	↓	↑	↑	Abnormal

Neurochemical Findings in the Influenza and PolyI:C Models

Since neurochemical alterations such as in the dopaminergic, glutamatergic, or serotonergic system are highly characteristic for the neurobiology of schizophrenia, some of such findings in the animal models should be reported here in detail. The efficacy of dopamine D2 receptor blocking drugs in the treatment of schizophrenia, as well as SPECT studies on neuroleptic naïve patients, suggests that dopamine hyperfunction in the ventral striatum and dopamine hypofunction in the prefontal cortex may be responsible for the positive symptomology of schizophrenia (Abi-Dargham et al., 2000, Abi-Dargham, 2002). Additionally, electrophysiological studies have suggested increased serotonergic function in schizophrenia (Juckel, Gallinat, Riedel et al., 2003, Juckel et al., 2008).

As mentioned above, viral infection causes deleterious effects on brain structure and function in mouse offspring following late first trimester (E9) and late second trimester (E18) administration of influenza virus. Neurochemical analysis following infection on E18 using this model has revealed significantly altered levels of serotonin, 5-hydroxyindoleacetic acid, taurine, but not dopamine. In order to monitor these different patterns of monoamine expression in exposed offspring in more detail and to see if there are changes in the dopamine system at another time point, C57BL6J mice were infected with a sublethal dose of human influenza virus or sham-infected using vehicle solution on E16. Male offspring of the infected mice were collected at P0, P14, and P56, their brains removed and cerebellum dissected and flash frozen. Dopamine and serotonin levels were then measured using HPLC-ED technique. When compared to controls, there was a significant decrease in serotonin levels in the cerebella of virally exposed mice at P14. No differences in levels of dopamine were observed in exposed and control mice although there was a significant decrease in dopamine at P14 and P56 when compared to P0. This study (Winter et al., 2008) has shown that the serotonergic system is disrupted following prenatal viral infection potentially modeling disruptions that occur in patients with schizophrenia, but there was no significant effect on the dopaminergic system. In an additional study (Fatemi et al., 2008), microarray, qRT-PCR, DTI and MRI scanning, Western blotting, and neurochemical analysis were performed to detect differences in gene expression and brain atrophy. Expression of several genes associated with schizophrenia or autism including Sema3a, Trfr2, and Vldlr was found to be altered as were protein levels of Foxp2. E18 infection of C57BL6J mice with a sublethal dose of human influenza virus led to significant gene alterations in frontal, hippocampal, and cerebellar cortices of developing mouse progeny. Brain imaging revealed significant atrophy in several brain areas and white matter thinning in corpus callosum. Finally, neurochemical analysis revealed significantly altered levels of serotonin (P14, P35), 5-hydroxyindoleacetic acid (P14), and taurine (P35), but again not concerning the dopaminergic or the glutamatergic system (Figure 1).

In the established mouse model mimicking viral-like infection with PolyI:C, we were able to show much clearer neurochemical effects in one study (Winter et al., 2008) as in the influenza model. Prenatal infection-induced changes in brain and behavioral functions are found to be associated with multiple changes at the neurochemical level. Pregnant dams on gestation day 9 were exposed to viral mimetic polyriboinosinic-polyribocytidilic acid (PolyI:C, 5 mg/kg i.v.) or vehicle treatment, and basal neurotransmitter levels were then compared in the adult brains of animals born to PolyI:C- or vehicle-treated mothers by high-performance liquid chromatography on postmortem tissue. We found that prenatal immune activation significantly increased the levels of dopamine and its major metabolites in the lateral globus pallidus and prefrontal cortex, while at the same time it decreased serotonin and its metabolite in the hippocampus, nucleus accumbens, and lateral globus pallidus. In addition, a specific reduction of the inhibitory amino acid taurine in the hippocampus was noted in prenatally PolyI:C-exposed offspring relative to controls, whereas central glutamate and c-aminobutyric acid (GABA) content was largely unaffected by prenatal immune activation (Table 2). These results thus confirm that maternal immunological stimulation during early/middle pregnancy is sufficient to induce long-term changes in multiple neurotransmitter levels in the brains of adult offspring. This further supports the possibility that infection-mediated interference with early fetal brain development may predispose the developing organism to the emergence of neurochemical imbalances in adulthood, which may be critically involved in the precipitation of adult behavioral and pharmacological abnormalities after prenatal immune challenge.

Microglial Activation

According to the hypothesis declared above, a first own study (Juckel et al., 2011) was aimed to explore microglial activation in PolyI:C-exposed mice at postnatal day 30 quantitatively and qualitatively in comparison to NaCl exposed control animals in brain regions involved in the pathogenesis of schizophrenia (frontal cortex, hippocampus, and striatum). Female and male BALB/c mice were maintained under standard laboratory conditions by breeding. Mice were mated overnight, and the presence of vaginal plug marked that day as embryonic day 0. At embryonic day (ED) 9 pregnant mice were treated with intraperitoneal injections of PolyI:C at a single dose of 20 mg/kg. Control mice were given injections of sterile sodium chloride (0.9%). After this procedure pregnant mice were housed singly. Thirty days after birth, descendants were deeply anesthetized and transcardially perfused. Subsequently, 40-μm-thick sagittal sections were cut by using a vibratome. Fluorescence immunostaining was performed according to standard protocols (e.g., Ohsawa, Imai, Kanasawa, Sasaki, & Kohsaka, 2000). Brain sections were incubated with rabbit polyclonal anti-Iba1 antibody. In addition, a combined CD11b/Iba1 staining was performed to reveal the activation and immune competence

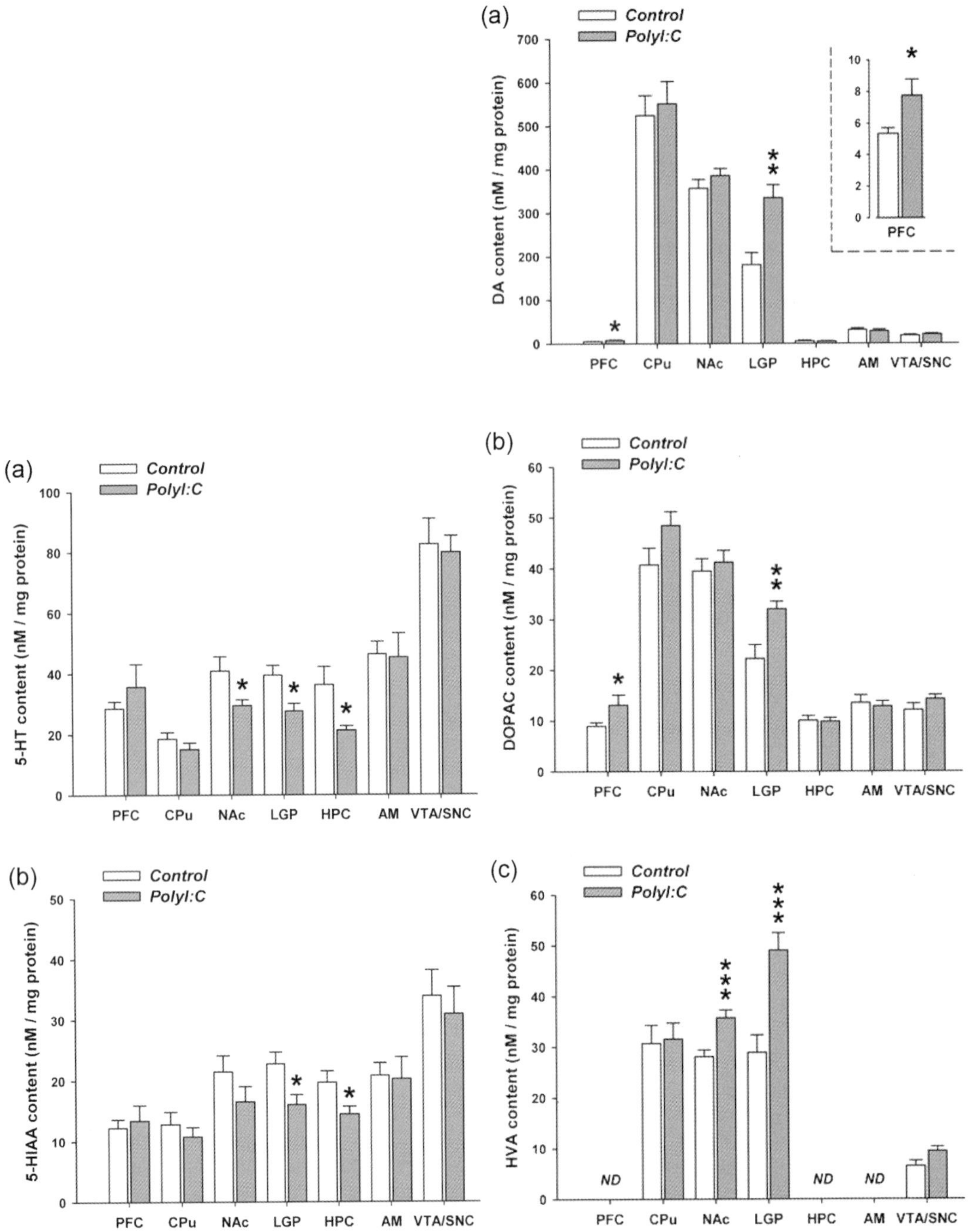

Figure 1. PolyI:C administration at day E9 and measurement of neurotransmitters at day P84 (taken from Winter et al., 2009).

of microglial cells. Immunostaining was performed in offspring from PolyI:C-treated mice and respective controls. Averaged values from two sagittal sections were taken at the medio-lateral position. Quantitative evaluation of Iba1-positive microglia cells was done in four brain areas: hippocampus, frontal cortex, striatum, and as a control region the occipital cortex. Furthermore, microglial branches and processes were analyzed by using a confocal microscope. PolyI:C treatment caused a significant increase in hippocampus and a significant increase in striatum. There were no significant effects of treatment in the frontal cortex as well as in the control region of the occipital cortex. The density of the Iba1-positive processes of the microglial cells was reduced in the brains of the descendants

Table 2. PolyI:C administration at day E9 and measurement of neurotransmitters at day P84 (taken from Winter et al., 2008)

	GABA	GLU	GABA	GLU
	CON		PolyI:C	
PFC	11.82 ± 1.24	89.33 ± 8.28	12.83 ± 1.12	88.53 ± 8.72
CPu	11.84 ± 1.13	70.05 ± 6.85	10.83 ± 0.86	64.65 ± 5.64
NAc	29.20 ± 3.14	60.53 ± 5.14	24.52 ± 2.64	61.82 ± 6.15
LGP	27.93 ± 3.36	52.43 ± 6.82	32.04 ± 4.12	52.85 ± 4.97
HPC	14.54 ± 2.47	64.82 ± 11.31	14.82 ± 1.45	64.54 ± 6.35
AM	26.51 ± 2.99	78.04 ± 10.14	25.22 ± 2.75	69.52 ± 10.21
VTA/SN	39.70 ± 6.03	46.43 ± 6.72	35.97 ± 4.77	41.21 ± 7.15

of the injected mothers as compared to the controls. In the control mice, Iba1-positive cells showed round or oval cell bodies with highly branched processes that formed a dense meshwork. In descendants of the mothers injected with PolyI:C, fine branches were largely diminished, particularly in hippocampus. Microglial cells of descendants from PolyI:C infected mothers exhibited significantly less branches and processes as compared to the control mice, which was supported by confocal microscopy showing reduced surface of processes in PolyI:C mice (Figure 2), suggesting that PolyI:C treatment of mothers caused a higher activation status in the offspring generation. Activated and immune competent status of microglial cells could also be demonstrated by combined CD11b/Iba1 staining. This study was able to demonstrate a higher number of activated microglia in the hippocampus and striatum of PolyI:C-exposed mice descendants at day 30 which is comparable to adolescence/early adulthood in a human being, a time window, in which first symptoms of schizophrenia appear or its first manifestation can be seen. The branches and processes of the microglial cells derived from PolyI:C-exposed mice were different to those of the control group. While microglial cells from control animals showed more highly branched arborization, indicative for a noninflammatory state of microglia, offspring from PolyI:C-treated mice were characterized by not or less branched cells, characteristic for an activated and inflammatory or phagocytic state of microglia (e.g., Shapiro, Perez, Foresti, Arisi, & Ribak, 2009; e.g., Stence, Waite, & Dailey, 2001). Activated microglia could lead to neuropil reduction with rarification of synapses, dendrites, and spines in patients with schizophrenic disorders due to a direct neurotoxic effect (e.g., NO, release of cytokines or free radicals) causing the well-known neuroanatomical changes in the early phases of this disease (e.g., Stehen, Mull, McClure, Hamer, & Lieberman, 2006; e.g., Witthaus et al., 2009) as well as the psychopathological symptoms and cognitive symptoms. Alternatively, microglial-derived mediators could lead to neurophysiological changes in the neuronal morphology. Given the duration of this activation, one may also consider negative effects on neural stem cell proliferation and intergration into the respective brain areas.

In a second study (Manitz et al., 2013), we have performed longitudinal observation across the life span concerning microglial activation in the PolyI:C model and have analyzed also data from PND10 and PND100 offsprings. There was no statistical difference between treatment groups concerning number of microglial cells per mm at PND10. At PND30, there was a significant higher number of microglial cells in all regions studied in descendants from Poly(I:C)-treated mothers: FrA ($p = .009$), CPu ($p = .005$), DG ($p = .009$), V1 ($p = .019$), with the exception of the M1. Interestingly, at PND100 a significant increase ($p = .023$) of microglial cell number was found only in the FrA of the offspring from Poly(I:C) injected dams. Thus, we were able to show a developmental

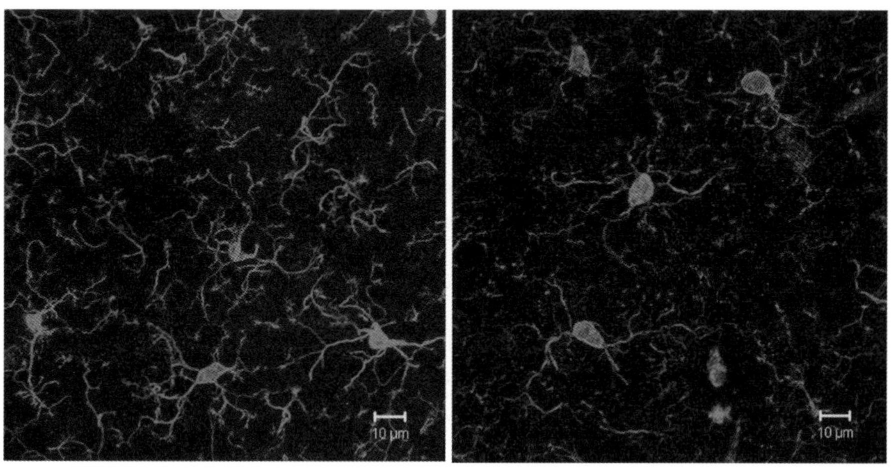

Figure 2. Confocal imaging of Iba1-stained microglial cell: Resting microglia in control versus activated microglial cell in PolyI:C animals (see Juckel et al., 2011).

dynamics of microglial activation in different brain regions in the inflammatory Poly(I:C) mouse model of schizophrenia. While mice pups displayed no microglial alterations in response to prenatal exposure to Poly(I:C), adolescent mice showed a significant increase in the number of microglial cells in frontal association cortex, ventral striatum, dentate gyrus of hippocampus, and secondary visual cortex. In contrast, in adult mice the immunological activation remains only within the frontal association cortex. These developmental dynamics of microglial activation in our animal model fit very well to the well-known findings about course and pathogenesis of schizophrenia. In mice pups (PND10), the process leading to schizophrenia-related pathophysiological and behavioral changes is still "sleeping." However, in adolescent mice (PND30), a huge immunological reaction with activation of microglial cells occurs. Adolescence in human beings is the time of fully manifested disease, which slows down with further adulthood. Actually, in adult descendants of Poly(I:C)-treated mice the immunological process seems to remain active only within the frontal association cortex. This could be related to the known cognitive deficits and negative symptoms remaining during the late course of schizophrenia (Howes, Fusar-Poli, Bloomfield, Selvaraj, & McGuire, 2012). Thus, these developmental dynamics of microglial activation in our animal model point to an important role of microglia during life span in schizophrenia.

Conclusion

Maternal infection during pregnancy is an environmental risk factor for descendants to develop severe neuropsychiatric disorders such as schizophrenia. The course of schizophrenia with lifelong remissions and relapses has been widely debated. Immunological processes interfering with brain development are discussed as one cause of schizophrenia. There are excellent and well-validated inflammational-immunological animal models of this disease with an early inflammational signal such as influenza virus or PolyI:C during pregnancy and the following immunological activation with immune competent cells such as lymphocytes and microglia as well as immunological relevant molecules such as cytokines/interleukins. They mimic a huge range of behavioral and neurobiological characteristics similarly to patients with schizophrenia. In own studies within the PolyI:C model, we were able to demonstrate an increased number of microglial cells during the life span, especially during adolescence. It can be hypothesized that these cells contribute to disease pathogenesis and may actively be involved in the well-known gray matter loss in frontal and temporal brain areas as well as other related neurobiological changes such as, for example, neurochemical alteration mainly in the dopaminergic system, which we were also able to demonstrate in these inflammational animal models. Thus, these animal models can be used to understand the pathophysiology of schizophrenia better especially concerning the interaction of immune activation, inflammation, and neurodegeneration. Furthermore, this should lead to the development of anti-inflammational and supportive immunological treatment options and of preventive interventions. In the following years, the molecular mechanism should be studied as to how microglial cells exhibit neurotoxic effects on the neuronal substrate. Hereby, the role of cytokines such as interleukin 6 (Ye & Johnson, 1999) or of free radicals such as NO (Fatemi et al., 2000) might become clearer.

References

Abi-Dargham, A. (2002). Recent evidence for dopamine abnormalities in schizophrenia. *European Psychiatry, 4*, 341–347.

Abi-Dargham, A., Rodenhiser, J., Printz, D., Zea-Ponce, Y., Gil, R., Kegeles, L. S., … Laruelle, M. (2000). Increased baseline occupancy of D2 receptors by dopamine in schizophrenia. *Proceedings of the National Academy of Sciences of the United States of America, 97*, 8104–8109.

Bayer, T. A., Buslei, R., Havas, L., & Falkai, P. (1999). Evidence for activation of microglia in patients with psychiatric illnesses. *Neuroscience Letters, 271*, 126–128.

Brown, A. S., Begg, M. D., Gravenstein, S., Schäfer, C. A., Wyatt, R. J., Bensahan, M., … Susser, E. S. (2004). Serologic evidence of prenatal influenza in the etiology of schizophrenia. *Archives of General Psychiatry, 61*, 774–780.

Cahn, W., Hulshoff Pol, H. E., Lems, E. B., van Haren, N. E., Schnack, H. G., van der Linden, J. A., … Kahn, R. S. (2002). Brain volume changes in first-episode schizophrenia: A 1-year follow-up study. *Archives of General Psychiatry, 59*, 1002–1010.

Doorduin, J., de Vries, E. F., Willemsen, A. T., de Groot, J. C., Dierckx, R. A., & Klein, H. C. (2009). Neuroinflammation in schizophrenia-related psychosis: A PET study. *European Journal of Nuclear Medicine, 50*, 1801–1807. doi: 10.2967/jnumed.109.066647

Falkai, P., Schneider-Axmann, T., Honer, W. G., Vogeley, K., Schönell, H., Pfeiffer, U., … Tepest, R. (2003). Influence of genetic loading, obstetric complications and premorbid adjustment on brain morphology in schizophrenia: A MRI study. *European Archives of Psychiatry and Clinical Neuroscience, 253*, 92–99.

Fatemi, S. H., Cuadra, A. E., El-Fakahany, E. E., Sidwell, R. W., & Thuras, P. (2000). Prenatal viral infection causes alterations in nNOS expression in developing mouse brains. *Neuroreport, 11*, 1493–1496.

Fatemi, S. H., Earle, J., Kanodia, R., Kist, D., Emamian, E. S., Patterson, P. H., … Sidwell, R. (2002). Prenatal viral infection leads to pyramidal cell atrophy and macrocephaly in adulthood: Implications for genesis of autism and schizophrenia. *Cellular and Molecular Neurobiology, 22*, 25–33.

Fatemi, S. H., Emamian, E. S., Kist, D., Sidwell, R. W., Nakajima, K., Akhter, P., … Bailey, K. (1999). Defective corticogenesis and reduction in Reelin immunoreactivity in cortex and hippocampus of prenatally infected neonatal mice. *Molecular Psychiatry, 4*, 145–154.

Fatemi, S. H., Halt, A. R., Stary, J. M., Kanodia, R., Schulz, C., & Realmuto, G. R. (2002). Glutamic acid decarboxylase 65 and 67 kDa proteins are reduced in autistic parietal and cerebellar cortices. *Biological Psychiatry, 52*, 805–810.

Fatemi, S. H., Reutiman, T. J., Folsom, T. D., Huang, H., Oishi, K., Mori, S., & Juckel, G. (2008). Maternal infection leads to abnormal gene regulation and brain atrophy in mouse offspring: Implications for genesis of neurodevelopmental disorders. *Schizophrenia Research, 99*, 56–70.

Fatemi, S. H., Sidwell, R., Akhter, P., Sedgewick, J., Thuras, P., Bailey, K., & Kist, D. (1998). Human influenza viral infection in utero increases nNOS expression in hippocampi of neonatal mice. *Synapse, 29*, 84–88.

Fatemi, S. H., Sidwell, R., Kist, D., Akhter, P., Meltzer, H. Y., Bailey, K., & Sedgwick, J. (1998). Differential expression of synaptosome-associated protein 25 kDa [SNAP-25] in hippocampi of neonatal mice following exposure to human influenza virus in utero. *Brain Research, 800*, 1–9.

Gaughran, F. (2002). Immunity and schizophrenia: Autoimmunity, cytokines, and immune responses. *International Review of Neurobiology, 52*, 275–302.

Heinz, A., Romero, B., Gallinat, J., Juckel, G., & Weinberger, D. R. (2003). Molecular brain imaging and the neurobiology and genetics of schizophrenia. *Pharmacopsychiatry, 36*, 152–157.

Heinz, A., Saunders, R. C., Kolachana, B. S., Jones, D. W., Gorey, J. G., Bachevalier, J., & Weinberger, D. R. (1999). Striatal dopamine receptors and transporters in monkeys with neonatal temporal limbic damage. *Synapse, 32*, 71–79.

Heinz, A., & Weinberger, D. (2000). Schizophrenie: Die neurobiologische Entwicklungshypothese. In H. Helmchen, F. Henn, & H. Lauter (Eds.), *Psychiatrie der Gegenwart 5* [Psychiatry of the present 5] (pp. 89–104). Berlin, Germany: Springer.

Howes, O. D., Fusar-Poli, P., Bloomfield, M., Selvaraj, S., & McGuire, P. (2012). From the prodrome to chronic schizophrenia: The neurobiology underlying psychotic symptoms and cognitive impairments. *Current Pharmaceutical Design, 18*, 459–465.

Juckel, G., Gallinat, J., Riedel, M., Sokullu, S., Schulz, C., Möller, H. J., … Hegerl, U. (2003). Serotonergic dysfunction in schizophrenia assessed by the loudness dependence measure of primary auditory cortex evoked activity. *Schizophrenia Research, 64*, 115–124.

Juckel, G., Gudlowski, Y., Müller, D., Ozgürdal, S., Brüne, M., Gallinat, J., … Meisenzahl, E. M. (2008). Loudness dependence of the auditory evoked N1/P2 component as an indicator of serotonergic dysfunction in patients with schizophrenia – a replication study. *Psychiatry Research, 158*, 79–82.

Juckel, G., Manitz, M. P., Brüne, M., Friebe, A., Heneka, M. T., & Wolf, R. J. (2011). Microglial activation in a neuroinflammational animal model of schizophrenia – a pilot study. *Schizophrenia Research, 131*, 96–100.

Juckel, G., Müller-Schubert, A., Gaebel, W., & Hegerl, U. (1996). Residual symptoms and P300 in schizophrenic outpatients. *Psychiatry Research, 65*, 23–32.

Juckel, G., Reischies, F. M., Müller-Schubert, A., Vogel, A. C., Gaebel, W., & Hegerl, U. (1994). Ventricle size and P300 in schizophrenia. *European Archives of Psychiatry and Clinical Neuroscience, 243*, 352–354.

Juckel, G., Sass, L., & Heinz, A. (2003). Anhedonia, self-experience in schizophrenia, and implications for treatment. *Pharmacopsychiatry, 3*, 176–180.

Kreutzberg, G. W. (1996). Microglia: A sensor for pathological events in the CNS. *Trends in Neuroscience, 19*, 312–318.

Limosin, F., Rouillon, F., Payan, C., Cohen, J. M., & Strub, N. (2003). Prenatal exposure to influenza as a risk factor for adult schizophrenia. *Acta Psychiatrica Scandinavia, 107*, 331–335.

Manitz, M. P., Esslinger, M., Wachholz, S., Plümper, J., Friebe, A., Juckel, G., & Wolf, R. (2013). The role of microglia during life span in neuropsychiatric disease – an animal study. *Schizophrenia Research, 143*, 221–222. doi: 10.1016/j.schres.2012.10.028

Mathalon, D. H., Sullivan, E. V., Lim, K. O., & Pfefferbaum, A. (2001). Progressive brain volume changes and the clinical course of schizophrenia in men: A longitudinal magnetic resonance imaging study. *Archives of General Psychiatry, 58*, 148–157.

Mednick, S. A., Machon, R. A., Huttunen, M. O., & Bonett, D. (1988). Adult schizophrenia following prenatal exposure to an influenza epidemic. *Archives of General Psychiatry, 45*, 189–192.

Meyer, U. (2014). Prenatal poly(i:C) exposure and other developmental immune activation models in rodent systems. *Biological Psychiatry, 75*, 307–315.

Meyer, U., & Feldon, J. (2010). Epidemiology-driven neurodevelopmental animal models of schizophrenia. *Progress in Neurobiology, 90*, 285–326. doi: 10.1016/j.pneurobio.2009.10.018

Meyer, U., Nyffeler, M., Engler, A., Urwyler, A., Schedlowski, M., Knuesel, I., … Feldon, J. (2006). The time of prenatal immune challenge determines the specificity of inflammation-mediated brain and behavioral pathology. *Journal of Neuroscience, 26*, 4752–4762.

Monji, A., Kato, T., & Kanba, S. (2009). Cytokines and schizophrenia: Microglia hypothesis of schizophrenia. *Psychiatry and Clinical Neurosciences, 63*, 257–265.

Müller, N., & Ackenheil, M. (1998). Psychoneuroimmunology and the cytokine action in the CNS: Implications for psychiatric disorders. *Progress in Neuropsychopharmacology & Biological Psychiatry, 22*, 1–33.

Müller, N., Dobmeier, P., Empl, M., Riedel, M., Schwarz, M., & Ackenheil, M. (1997). Soluble IL-6 receptors in the serum and cerebrospinal fluid of paranoid schizophrenic patients. *European Psychiatry, 12*, 294–299. doi: 10.1016/S0924-9338(97)84789-X

Müller, N., Riedel, M., Scheppach, C., Brandstätter, B., Sokullu, S., Krampe, K., … Schwarz, M. J. (2002). Beneficial antipsychotic effects of celecoxib add-on therapy compared to risperidone alone in schizophrenia. *The American Journal of Psychiatry, 159*, 1029–1034.

Müller, N., Schlesinger, B. C., Hadjamu, M., Riedel, M., Schwarz, M., Ackenheil, M., … Gruber, R. (1998). Increased frequency of CD8 positive gamma/delta T-lymphocytes (CD8+ gamma/delta+) in unmedicated schizophrenic patients: Relation to impairment of the blood-brain barrier and HLA-DPA*02011. *Schizophrenia Research, 32*, 69–71.

Munk-Jørgensen, P., & Ewald, H. (2001). Epidemiology in neurobiological research: Exemplified by the influenza-schizophrenia theory. *The British Journal of Psychiatry: Supplement, 40*, 530–532.

Munn, N. A. (2000). Microglia dysfunction in schizophrenia: An integrative theory. *Medical Hypotheses, 54*, 198–202.

Ohsawa, K., Imai, Y., Kanasawa, H., Sasaki, Y., & Kohsaka, S. (2000). Involvement of Iba1 in membrane ruffling and phagocytosis of macrophages/microglia. *Journal of Cell Science, 113*, 3073–3084.

Pantelis, C., Velakoulis, D., McGorry, P. D., Wood, S. J., Suckling, J., Phillips, L. J., … McGuire, P. K. (2003). Neuroanatomical abnormalities before and after onset of psychosis: A cross-sectional and longitudinal MRI comparison. *Lancet, 361*, 281–288.

Radewicz, K., Garey, L. J., Gentleman, S. M., & Reynolds, R. (2000). Increase in HLA-DR immunoreactive microglia in frontal and temporal cortex of chronic schizophrenics. *Journal of Neuropathology & Experimental Neurology, 59*, 137–150.

Rami, A. (2003). Ischemic neuronal death in the rat hippocampus: The calpain-calpastatin-caspase hypothesis. *Neurobiology Disorder, 13*, 75–88.

Rothermundt, M., Arolt, V., & Bayer, T. A. (2001). Review of immunological and immunopathological findings in schizophrenia. *Brain Behavior and Immunity, 15*, 319–339.

Scherk, H., Vogeley, K., & Falkai, P. (2003). Die Bedeutung von Interneuronen bei affektiven und schizophrenen Erkrankungen [The importance of interneurons in affective and schizophrenic disorders]. *Fortschritte der Neurologie – Psychiatrie, 71*, 27–32.

Shapiro, L. A., Perez, Z. D., Foresti, M. L., Arisi, G. M., & Ribak, C. E. (2009). Morphological and ultrastructural features of Iba1-immunolabeled microglial cells in the hippocampal dentate gyrus. *Brain Research, 1266*, 29–36.

Shi, L., Fatemi, S. H., Sidwell, R. W., & Patterson, P. H. (2003). A mouse model of mental illness: Maternal influenza infection causes behavioural and pharmacological abnormalities in the offspring. *Journal of Neuroscience, 23*, 297–302.

Stehen, R. G., Mull, C., McClure, R., Hamer, R. M., & Lieberman, J. A. (2006). Brain volume in first-episode schizophrenia: Systematic review and meta-analysis of magnetic resonance imaging studies. *The British Journal of Psychiatry, 188*, 510–518.

Stence, N., Waite, M., & Dailey, M. E. (2001). Dynamics of microglial activation: A confocal time-lapse analysis in hippocampal slices. *Glia, 33*, 256–266.

Takei, N., Lewis, S., Jones, P., Harvey, I., & Murray, R. M. (1996). Prenatal exposure to influenza and increased cerebrospinal fluid spaces in schizophrenia. *Schizophrenia Bulletin, 22*, 521–534.

van Berckel, B. N., Bossong, M. G., Boellaard, R., Kloet, R., Schuitemaker, A., Caspers, E., … Kahn, R. S. (2008). Microglia activation in recent-onset schizophrenia: A quantitative (R)-[11C]PK11195 positron emission tomography study. *Biological Psychiatry, 64*, 820–822.

Weinberger, D. R. (1995). From neuropathology to neurodevelopment. *Lancet, 346*, 552–557.

Winter, C., Djodari-Irani, A., Sohr, R., Morgenstern, R., Feldon, J., Juckel, G., & Meyer, U. (2009). Prenatal immune activation leads to multiple changes in basal neurotransmitter levels in the adult brain: Implications for brain disorders of neurodevelopmental origin such as schizophrenia. *The International Journal of Neuropsychopharmacology, 12*, 513–524.

Winter, C., Reutiman, T. J., Folsom, T. D., Sohr, R., Wolf, R. J., Juckel, G., & Fatemi, S. H. (2008). Dopamine and serotonin levels following prenatal viral infection in mouse-implications for psychiatric disorders such as schizophrenia and autism. *European Neuropsychopharmacology, 18*, 712–716.

Witthaus, H., Kaufmann, C., Bohner, G., Özgürdal, S., Gudlowski, Y., Gallinat, J., … Juckel, G. (2009). Gray matter abnormalities in subjects at ultra-high risk for schizophrenia and first-episode schizophrenic patients. *Psychiatry Research, 173*, 163–169. doi: 10.1016/j.pscychresns.2008.08.002

Ye, S. M., & Johnson, R. W. (1999). Increased interleukin-6 expression by microglia from brain of aged mice. *Journal of Neuroimmunolgy, 93*, 139–148.

Georg Juckel

Department of Psychiatry
Ruhr University Bochum
LWL University Hospital
Alexandrinenstr. 1-3
44791 Bochum
Germany
Tel. +49 234 5077-1100
Fax +49 234 5077-1119
E-mail georg.juckel@rub.de

Original Article

Phosphoinositide-Dependent Protein Kinase 1 (PDK1)

Impact on Schizophrenia Risk and Endophenotype Profile

Undine E. Lang,[1] Teresa F. Ackermann,[2] David Wolfer,[3] Florian Schubert,[4] Reinhard Sohr,[5] Heide Hörtnagl,[6] Florian Lang,[2] and Juergen Gallinat[7]

[1]Department of Psychiatry and Psychotherapy, University of Basel, Switzerland, [2]Department of Physiology I, University of Tuebingen, Germany, [3]Institute of Anatomy, University of Zurich and Department of Biology, ETH Zurich, Switzerland, [4]Physikalisch-Technische Bundesanstalt, Berlin, Germany, [5]Department of Pharmacology, Charité University Medicine Berlin, Germany, [6]Department of Pharmacology, University of Innsbruck, Austria, [7]Department of Psychiatry and Psychotherapy, University Hospital Hamburg, Germany

Abstract. Phosphatidylinositol-3-kinase (PI3K) signaling influences susceptibility to virus infections, anoxia, obstetric complications, and cancer; which are changed in patients with schizophrenia and their first degree relatives. Therefore PI3K signaling might have impact on the pathophysiology of schizophrenia. PI3K signaling crucially involves phosphoinositide-dependent protein kinase (PDK1). Increased anxiety behavior is observed in PDK1 hypomorphic mice. Here we show enhanced prevalence of schizophrenia in carriers of the PDK1 CC genotype in human beings. Moreover, decreased parietal P300 amplitude, which is a well-studied schizophrenic endophenotype, was observed in PDK1 CC carriers. Glutamate and glutamine concentrations are increased in the frontal lobe of PDK1 dysmorphic mice and human CC individuals. Our results demonstrate that the PDK1 CC genotype is associated with increased risk to develop schizophrenia, a typical endophenotype profile observed in the disease and modified neurotransmitter concentrations in brain regions associated with the disease.

Keywords: Schizophrenia, psychosis, phenotype

Schizophrenia is a severe psychiatric illness with complex etiology and lifetime prevalence of approximately 0.4% worldwide. Family, twin, and adoption studies have consistently demonstrated a genetic component of schizophrenia, together with developmental and environmental influences. According to current pathophysiological models the disease is the cognitive, perceptual, and behavioral outcome of subtle alterations in brain development occurring long before clinical symptoms evolve and involve glutamatergic, dopaminergic, and γ-aminobutyric acidergic systems (Lang, Puls, Müller, Strutz-Seebohm, & Gallinat, 2007).

The phosphatidylinositol-3-kinase (PI3K) signaling pathway regulates hippocampal proliferation, differentiation, and survival, fosters the development of dendrite size and shape, and induces functional synapses in neuronal cells (Kumar, Zhang, Swank, Kunz, & Wu, 2005; Martin-Pena et al., 2006; Peltier, O'Neill, & Schaffer, 2007). Neurotrophins require a functional PI3K pathway in cell body and distal axons to promote neuronal survival (Brunet, Datta, & Greenberg, 2001). Accordingly, this pathway has been implicated in the pathophysiology of schizophrenia (Jagannathan et al., 2010; Kalkman, 2006) and relevant genes expressed in this signaling pathway appear to be associated with the disease (Arguello & Gogos, 2008; Emamian, Hall, Birnbaum, Karayiorgou, & Gogos, 2004; Ikeda et al., 2004; Schwab et al., 2005). Treatment with the antipsychotic drugs haloperidol, risperidone, and clozapine ameliorates the purported dysfunction of the pathway (Kalkman, 2006). Both pharmacological inhibition and genetic manipulation of PI3K-dependent signaling demonstrate that PI3K signals via phosphatidylinositide-dependent kinase 1 (PDK1). Therefore, PDK1 is a direct downstream effector of PI3K (Vanhaesebroeck & Alessi, 2000) and plays a central role in activating other downstream processes, including cell proliferation, survival, and differentiation (Mora, Komander, van Aalten, & Alessi, 2004).

We recently observed that PDK1 deficiency in mice increases anxiety, which is a core feature of schizophrenia

DOI: 10.1027/2151-2604/a000217

(Ackermann et al., 2008). In the present study we explore, whether PDK1 is involved in the development of endophenotypal hallmarks of schizophrenia, the occurrence of the disease itself, changes in neurotransmission, and behavioral alterations in men and mice.

Material and Methods

Subjects

The study was approved by the Ethics Committee of the Charité University Medicine Berlin. Nine hundred fifty-one subjects, among them 540 healthy volunteers and 411 acute schizophrenic patients were recruited. All participants of the study gave written informed consent and were included only if both parents were of German descent and if three out of four grandparents were of the same descent.

All healthy subjects were free of medical, neurological, and psychiatric disorders as determined in personal interviews (Mini-International Neuropsychiatric Interview; Sheehan et al., 1998) performed by a psychiatrist. Subjects with a family history (first degree) of axis I disorder were excluded from participation. Further methodological details have been published elsewhere (Gallinat et al., 2010).

The 411 schizophrenic patients were recruited in the psychiatric department, Charité University Medicine Berlin. Diagnosis was confirmed on the basis of the Structured Clinical Interview for the Diagnostic and Statistical Manual of Mental Disorders (Spitzer, Williams, Gibbon, & First, 1992).

SNP Genotyping

Genomic DNA was extracted from anticoagulated venous blood samples using a salting out method (Miller, Dykes, & Polesky, 1988). PDPK1 SNP rs1005273 was genotyped by Illumina (Illumina, Inc., San Diego, CA).

P300 Recording and Analysis

The P300 amplitude was determined as the most positive amplitude between 250 and 500 ms poststimulus automatically by the analysis software (Brain Vision Analyzer Version 1.05) at the electrode positions Fz (frontal), Cz (frontocentral), and Pz (parietal), each referred to linked mastoids. A visual inspection of the results was performed to control for erroneous determinations (Gallinat et al., 2007).

MR Spectroscopy

Magnetic resonance measurements in human beings were carried out on a 3-Tesla scanner (MEDSPEC 30/100; Bruker Biospin, Ettlingen, Germany) with a circularly polarized head coil. After automated global shim of the linear, xz, z^2, and x^2-y^2 field components, T_1-weighted images (modified driven equilibrium Fourier transform, MDEFT) were acquired. The MR spectra were recorded from $2.5 \times 4 \times 2$ cm^3 voxels including the ACC and from $2 \times 3 \times 2$ cm^3 voxels including the left hippocampus of the volunteer brains.

For metabolite quantification we closely followed a method published previously (Schubert, Gallinat, Seifert, & Rinneberg, 2004). After manual shimming to water linewidths (full width at half maximum, FWHM) of 7–9 Hz and 6–7 Hz for the hippocampus and ACC voxels, respectively, and determination of the radiofrequency power needed for a 90° excitation pulse, calibration of water suppression was carried out, followed by acquisition of spectra with point resolved spectroscopy (PRESS). To obtain one MR spectrum, eight subspectra of 16 phase cycled scans each were recorded with $T_R = 3$ s and $T_E = 80$ ms, giving 128 averages. Subsequently the water suppression pulses were switched off to acquire a water-unsuppressed spectrum ($n = 8$). Before further processing, the eight individual metabolite subspectra were corrected for eddy currents with the water-unsuppressed spectrum and automatically frequency aligned to correct for frequency shifts during the scan. The spectral linewidth (FWHM) values of the metabolite resonances are estimated by the used fitting procedure (described in following text); mean FWHM (*SD*) (in Hz) were 4.9 (.6) for the ACC voxel and 6.6 (.9) for the hippocampus voxel and thus below the minimum acceptable line width for high-precision MR spectroscopy suggested recently (Kreis, Ernst, & Ross, 1993). Spectra were quantified with a program package that relies on a time domain-frequency domain fitting procedure and involves inclusion of phantom basis spectra and prior knowledge into the fit (Elster et al., 2005; Kreis et al., 1993). To account for features of the baseline, which was not entirely flat at the chosen T_E of 80 ms, the fitting procedure routinely includes estimation of the baseline nonparametrically by regularization. Metabolite glutamate amplitudes returned by the fitting procedure were corrected for different coil loading by the phantoms and the individual subject's head (principle of reciprocity) (Danielsen & Henriksen, 1994) and for relaxation effects, using relaxation times from previous work (Jagannathan et al., 2010) and assuming no differences in relaxation behavior between the subjects.

The in vivo concentrations were corrected for the content of cerebrospinal fluid (CSF) of the voxels studied, as derived from segmentation of the T_1-weighted images with spm2 (Ashburner & Friston, 1997). Providing the highest retest reliability (Kreis et al., 1993), a pixel was classified depending on which spm2 tissue classification had the greatest probability.

Statistical Analyses

Effects of the genotype on brain metabolites were analyzed with multiple analysis of variance (MANOVA). Analyses were computed using statistical software (SPSS 14.0®). A type-I error rate of $p < .05$ was considered significant.

Animals

The generation and basic properties of PDK1 hypomorphic mice have been described earlier (Lawlor et al., 2002; Sandu et al., 2006). Genotyping was made by PCR on tail DNA using PDK1 and neo-R-specific primers as previously described (Vanhaesebroeck & Alessi, 2000). Mice had free access to standard mouse diet (Altromin, Langen, Germany) and tap water. All animal experiments were conducted according to the guidelines of the American Physiological Society and the German law for the welfare of animals and were approved by the local Animal Committee. For the present study, 12 PDK1 hypomorphic mice ($PDK1^{hm}$) and their wild type littermates ($n = 16$; $PDK1^{wt}$) were studied.

Housing and Handling

All animal procedures were approved by Swiss and Tuebingen animal welfare authorities. Mice were bred and housed at Tuebingen. One week before the experimental period, animals were transferred to the Institute of Anatomy in Zürich where they were single housed in standard type II mouse cages and maintained at a 12:12 hr inverted cycle with lights on between 8 p.m. and 8 a.m. Standard mouse chow, water, and nesting material were available ad libitum.

Dissection of the Brains and Homogenization Procedure

After decapitation, the brains were rapidly removed, immediately frozen on dry ice, and stored at −80 °C until use. For dissection, the frozen brains were placed on a cold plate providing a temperature between −10 and −12 °C. At this temperature the brain tissue was in a semi-frozen state with well-preserved anatomical structure. The amygdala/piriform cortex was cut out using the rhinal fissure as landmark. The olfactory bulb was dissected along the basis of the frontal cortex. Each tissue sample was homogenized by ultrasonication in 40–80 volumes of distilled water. One hundred fifty microliters of the homogenate was added to an equal volume of 0.2 M perchloric acid and centrifuged at 25,000 g for 20 min at 4 °C. Dopamine (DA) was measured in the supernatant. For amino acid analysis, 20 μL of the homogenate was added to 80 μL methanol and centrifuged at 25,000 g for 20 min at 4 °C. The supernatant was diluted 1:30 with distilled water.

Determination of Monoamines and Metabolites

NA was measured by HPLC with electrochemical detection after extraction to alumina, according to Felice, Felice, and Kissinger (1978) with minor modifications (Sperk, 1982; Sperk, Berger, Hörtnagl, & Hornykiewicz, 1981).

Determination of Amino Acids

Glutamate, γ-aminobutyric acid (GABA), glutamine, and taurine were determined using methods described previously (Piepponen & Skujins, 2001). In brief, amino acids were precolumn derivatized with o-phthalaldehyde-2-mercaptoethanol using a refrigerated autoinjector and then separated on a HPLC column (ProntoSil C18 ace-EPS) at a flow rate of .6 mL/min and a column temperature of 40 °C. The mobile phase was acetonitrile 50 mmol/mL sodium acetate solution pH = 5.7 in a linear gradient from 5% to 21% acetonitrile. Derivatized amino acids were detected by their fluorescence at 450 nm and excitation at 330 nm.

Fear Conditioning

Four mice were tested in parallel in an Actimetrics FreezeFrame video-based Conditioned Fear System (www.actimetrics.com). The conditioning chambers (175 mm deep × 180 mm wide × 280 mm high) are enclosed in ventilated and sound-attenuated cabinets and have a floor consisting of stainless steel rods permitting the application of current. The *training* session consisted of a 60 s pre-exposure to the training context immediately followed by three 60 s training trials consisting of a 2,500 Hz 85 dB tone (CS) lasting 30 s, co-terminating with a 2 s 0.25 A foot shock (US), and followed by a 30 s interval. To assess memory consolidation 24 h after training, the mice were re-exposed to the training chamber for 120 s without activation of the CS or US (*context test*). Thereafter the floor of the conditioning chamber was covered with plastic and some bedding material and a pebble were added. The mice were pre-exposed to this modified context for 60 s which was immediately followed by a 60 s CS presentation (*tone test*).

Freezing (absence of movement aside from respiration) was quantified automatically by the FreezeFrame software subtracting subsequent images recorded by the ceiling-mounted IR video cameras in the conditioning chambers. Bouts of 1.0 s were used to define % freezing and movement thresholds were set at 20 (training and context test) or 8 units (tone test). The training effect was evaluated by comparison of % freezing during the last training cycle with freezing during the first CS presentation plus the last 30 s of pre-exposure. The US-context association was assessed by comparing % freezing during pre-exposure with % freezing during the context test. The US-CS association (consolidation) was evaluated by comparing % freezing during the pre-CS and CS phases of the tone test. Additional measures were: % freezing during context pre-exposure (unconditioned freezing to the training context), % freezing during the first tone presentation (unconditioned freezing to the tone), % freezing during the pre-CS phase of the tone test (generalized freezing to the new context).

Results and Discussion

We found that the occurrence of schizophrenia is increased in carriers of the PDK1 CC genotype variant in human beings (n = 951; df = 2, χ^2 = 9.6, p = .008; see Figure 1).

Deficits in parietal P300 generation in schizophrenia were first reported in the 1970s and have been extensively replicated since then, with an observed effect size deficit of approximately 0.89 across studies (Jeon & Polich, 2003; Waters, 2009). The P300 is not only a biological marker of the genetic risk of suffering a psychotic episode but determines the type and gravity of the symptoms of the disease, as well as the degree of structural deterioration of the patient. Patients with first-rank symptoms have significantly reduced amplitudes and longer latencies on the P300, as compared to controls (Wirth et al., 2011). Comparing a sample of 350 schizophrenic patients and 201 healthy age-matched controls we found decreased P300 amplitudes at Pz electrode in the patients (F = 59.958, df = 1, p < .0001; see Figure 1b). The PDK1 genotype was significantly associated with the P300 amplitude (F = 3.858, df = 1, p = .022) with some evidence for a diagnosis by genotype interaction (F = 2.873, df = 2, p = .057). Contrast analysis revealed significant smaller P300 amplitude in CC compared to CT individuals (p = .007) (see Figure 1).

The association between genotype and psychopathology was calculated using a recently published analysis of the PANSS factor structure based on an empirical factor analysis (Wirth et al., 2011). A significant association between genotype and factor "depression" was observed (F = 4.058, df = 2, p = .018) with higher depression scores in the CC group compared with the CT individuals (Figure 2c). At least in animals PI3K signaling has been implicated in depressive behavior (Ackermann, Kempe, Lang, & Lang, 2010; Budni et al., 2011). No significant association was observed for the factors "positive" symptoms, "negative" symptoms, "excitement," and "cognition" ($p \geq .05$). These observations indicate PDK1 to play a role for specific psychopathologic domains of the disease. In a further experiment we examined if PDK1 influences neurotransmitter concentrations in brain areas relevant for schizophrenia since glutamatergic abnormalities have been observed with magnetic resonance spectroscopy (van Elst et al., 2005) and PI3K plays a pivotal role in the induction of hippocampal NMDA- or group I metabotropic glutamate receptor 1 (mGluR1)-dependent long-term potentiation (Kim et al., 2011).

In a single voxel MRS focusing on determination of absolute glutamate concentrations we observed a significant association between PDK1 genotype (CC vs. pooled

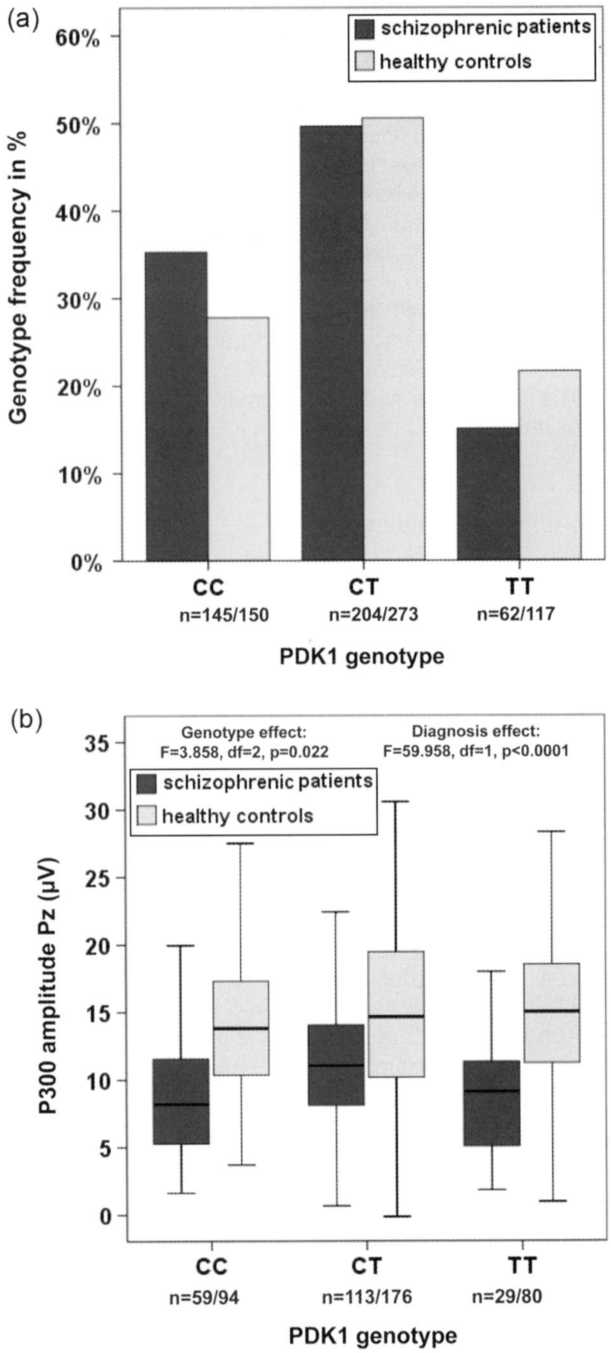

Figure 1. (a) Effect of genotype on the diagnosis of schizophrenia in patients (n = 411) and healthy controls (n = 540). CC genotype is more frequent in patients compared to healthy controls. (b) Effect of genotype on P300 amplitude (Pz electrode) in schizophrenic patients (n = 201) and healthy controls (n = 350). P300 is decreased in schizophrenic patients (F = 59.958, df = 1, p < .0001) and decreased in CC genotype carriers (F = 3.858, df = 2, p = .022).

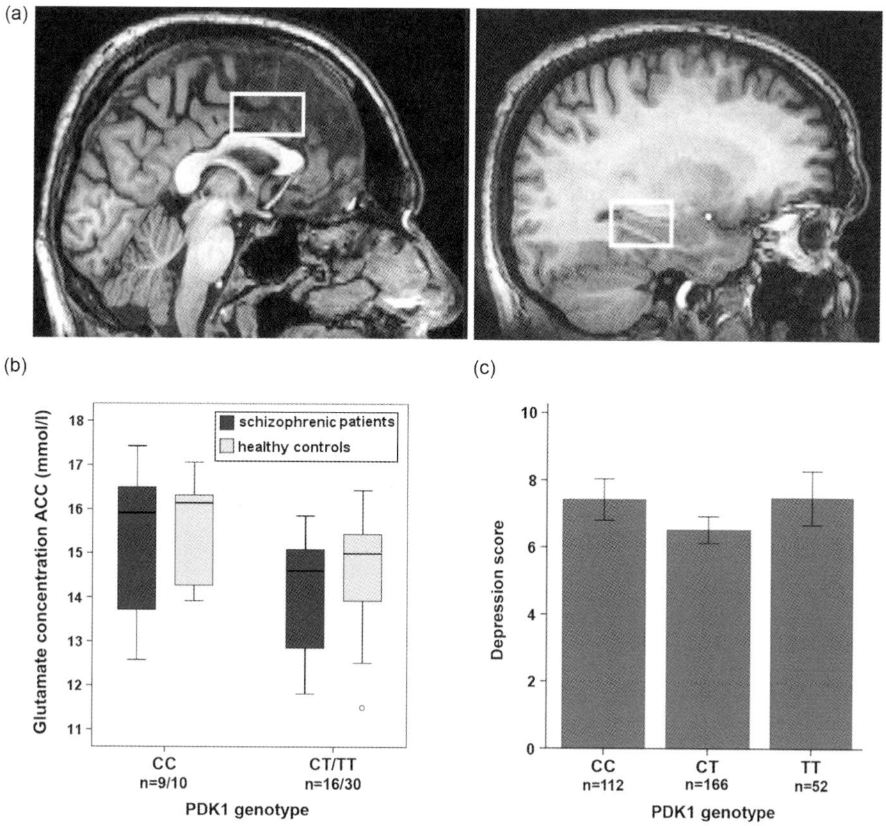

Figure 2. (a) Voxel positions shown on typical T1-weighted brain images; anterior cingulate cortex (ACC, left), hippocampus (right). (b) Boxplot of glutamate concentrations (mmol/L) measured in the ACC in schizophrenic patients (n = 25) and healthy controls (n = 40). Glutamate concentrations are higher in CC genotype subjects compared to the combined CT + TT genotypes. (c) Effect of genotype on the factor "depression" of the PANSS (± standard error).

CT/TT) and absolute glutamate concentration in the anterior cingulate cortex in a sample of 25 schizophrenic and 40 healthy control ($F = 7.429$, $df = 1$, $p = .008$; see Figure 2b). No differences between patients and controls were observed regarding glutamate concentration ($F = 2.096$, $df = 1$, $p = .153$).

In the animal experiment with PDK1 dysmorphic mice we found an increased glutamine concentration in the frontal cortex (Table 1A) as well as increased concentrations of glutamine, glutamate, and dopamine in the hippocampus (Table 1B). Moreover, increased glutamate concentrations were found in the hypothalamus (Table 1C).

In mice these differences were paralleled by behavioral differences, namely a significantly increased shock sensitivity in the fear-conditioning test in PDK1 dysmorphic mice (Figure 3). In the fear-conditioning paradigm, mice have to associate a conditioned stimulus such as the context or a tone, to an unconditional stimulus. The hippocampus is thought to govern primarily the processing of the contextual representation that will be associated with the unconditional stimuli, which is changed typically in schizophrenic patients.

The diminished activity of the PI3K pathway via PDK1 dysregulation provides an explanation for several of the diverse observations in schizophrenia. On the one hand, constitutive overactivation of this pathway increases cancer risk (Carnero, 2010). Consequently, the presumed hypoactivity of the PI3K cascade might provide a partial

Table 1. Neurotransmitter concentrations in the (A) frontal cortex (per mg tissue), (B) hippocampus (per mg tissue), (C) hypothalamus (per mg tissue) of mice with deficient phosphatidylinositol-3-kinase signaling (PDK1 hypomorphic mice) compared to wild type mice (WT)

	WT (n = 16)	PDK1 (n = 12)	Significance
	(A)		
GABA nmol	2.94 ± 0.13	2.91 ± 0.13	*ns*
Glutamate nmol	12.26 ± 0.32	12.53 ± 0.29	*ns*
Glutamine nmol	4.85 ± 0.14	6.29 ± 0.55	$p = .01$
Taurine nmol	13.22 ± 0.36	12.45 ± 0.41	*ns*
	(B)		
Dopamine pg	81.0 ± 11.6	164.2 ± 22.2	$p = .001$
GABA nmol	2.76 ± 0.05	2.88 ± 0.05	*ns*
Glutamate nmol	10.04 ± 0.2	11.06 ± 0.31	$p = .008$
Glutamine nmol	4.47 ± 0.09	6.4 ± 0.64	$p = .002$
Taurine nmol	10.93 ± 0.14	10.67 ± 0.37	*ns*
	(C)		
Dopamine pg	482.1 ± 29.2	480.8 ± 29.4	*ns*
DOPAC pg	85.6 ± 4	97.6 ± 10.5	*ns*
HVA pg	153.5 ± 7.2	148.5 ± 13.5	*ns*
GABA nmol	6.89 ± 0.1	7.01 ± 0.22	*ns*
Glutamine nmol	4.98 ± 0.08	6.65 ± 0.42	$p < .001$
Glutamate nmol	6.25 ± 0.15	7.00 ± 0.2	$p = .005$
Taurine nmol	5.25 ± 0.09	5.11 ± 0.23	*ns*

ANOVA Table for lvoc

	DF	Sum of Squares	Mean Square	F-Value	P-Value	Lambda	Power
grp	1	.011	.011	9.557	.0175	9.557	.762
sex	1	.002	.002	1.920	.2083	1.920	.217
grp * sex	1	.001	.001	.557	.4798	.557	.097
Residual	7	.008	.001				

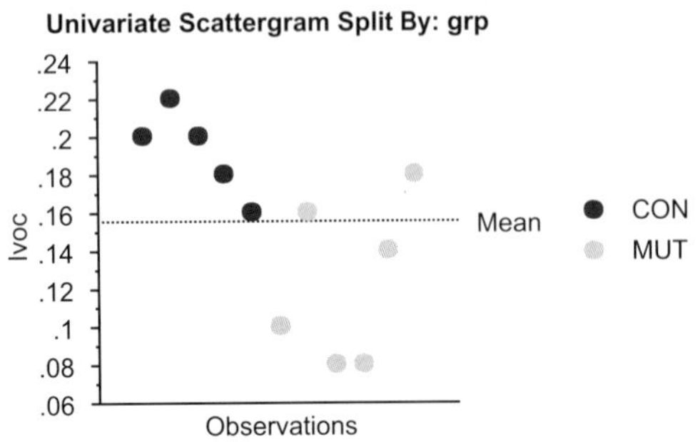

Figure 3. PDK 1 dysmorphic mice display an increased shock sensitivity in the fear conditioning test.

explanation for the remarkable epidemiological finding of a reduced cancer rate in schizophrenic patients and their first degree relatives (Catts, Catts, O'Toole, & Frost, 2008). Indeed, decreased occurrence of lung, colorectal, and prostate cancer in schizophrenic patients has been described by several authors (Altar et al., 2008). The reduction of cancer incidence in family members of schizophrenic patients suggests a genetic cause for the reduced cancer risk in schizophrenic patients.

Various factors have been discussed to parallel schizophrenic symptoms and treatment effects: insulin, insulin-like growth factor-1 (Lee, Lange, Ricken, Hellweg, & Lang, 2011; Venkatasubramanian, Chittiprol, Neelakantachar, Shetty, & Gangadhar, 2010), brain-derived neurotrophic factor (Lee et al., 2011), epidermal growth factor (Ikeda et al., 2008), neuregulin-1 (Nicodemus et al., 2010), erythropoietin (Wüstenberg et al., 2011), dysbindin (Dickman & Davis, 2009), and others. However, all these proteins lead to full enzymatic activity of PI3K and/or the phosphorylation of protein kinase B (PKB) (Nicodemus et al., 2010; Wyatt et al., 2006).

At present, dopamine D2 receptor antagonists remain the only used antipsychotic drugs and main pharmacological treatment of schizophrenia. Chronic treatment with these substances induces D2 receptor upregulation (Silvestri et al., 2000), which has been shown to be connected with inactivation of AKT (Lu & Dwyer, 2005). These observations are in line with direct in vitro observations that the second generation antipsychotic drugs olanzapine, quetiapine, and clozapine enhance the phosphorylation of AKT (Aubry, Schwald, Ballmann, & Karege, 2009). Olanzapine, clozapine, and lithium activate PKB and lead to glycogen synthase kinase-3 (GSK-3) phosphorylation (Aubry et al., 2009; Gould & Manji, 2005; Klein & Melton, 1996; Lu & Dwyer, 2005). GSK-3 is phosphorylated and thus inhibited by PKB kinases activated through the PI3K pathway (Lang et al., 2006; Shaw, Cohen, & Alessi, 1997).

In conclusion, according to our observations the PDK1 gene impacts P300 amplitude, a well studied biological hallmark of schizophrenia shown to be highly hereditable or driven by genetic variations and therefore regarded as endophenotype of schizophrenic patients. Moreover, we found an influence of PDK1 on glutamatergic neurotransmission in mice and men. Small-molecule inhibitors of the PI3K signaling network have been targeted as promising anticancer drugs but, according to the present observations might well induce schizophrenia-like, possibly dangerous side effects, to be monitored and treated in affected patients.

References

Ackermann, T. F., Hörtnagl, H., Wolfer, D. P., Colacicco, G., Lang, F., Sohr, R., ... Lang, U. E. (2008). Phosphatidylinositide dependent kinase deficiency increases anxiety and decreases GABA and serotonin abundance in the amygdala. *Cellular Physiology and Biochemistry, 22*, 735–744.

Ackermann, T. F., Kempe, D. S., Lang, F., & Lang, U. E. (2010). Hyperactivity and enhanced curiosity of mice expressing PKB/SGK-resistant glycogen synthase kinase-3 (GSK-3). *Cellular Physiology and Biochemistry, 25*, 775–786.

Altar, C. A., Hunt, R. A., Jurata, L. W., Webster, M. J., Derby, E., Gallagher, P., ... Leang, P. (2008). Insulin, IGF-1, and muscarinic agonists modulate schizophrenia-associated genes in human neuroblastoma cells. *Biological Psychiatry, 64*, 1077–1087.

Arguello, P. A., & Gogos, J. A. (2008). A signaling pathway AKTing up in schizophrenia. *The Journal of Clinical Investigation, 118*, 2018–2021.

Ashburner, J., & Friston, K. (1997). Multimodal image coregistration and partitioning – a unified framework. *NeuroImage, 6*, 209–217.

Aubry, J. M., Schwald, M., Ballmann, E., & Karege, F. (2009). Early effects of mood stabilizers on the Akt/GSK-3beta signaling pathway and on cell survival and proliferation. *Psychopharmacology (Berl), 205*, 419–429.

Brunet, A., Datta, S. R., & Greenberg, M. E. (2001). Transcription-dependent and -independent control of neuronal survival by the PI3K-Akt signaling pathway. *Current Opinion in Neurobiology, 11*, 297–305.

Budni, J., Lobato, K. R., Binfaré, R. W., Freitas, A. E., Costa, A. P., Saavedra, M. D., ... Rodrigues, A. L. (2011). Involvement of PI3K, GSK-3β and PPARγ in the antidepressant-like effect of folic acid in the forced swimming test in mice. *Journal of Psychopharmacology, 26*, 714–723. doi: 10.1177/0269881111424456

Carnero, A. (2010). The PKB/AKT pathway in cancer. *Current Pharmaceutical Design, 16*, 34–44.

Catts, V. S., Catts, S. V., O'Toole, B. I., & Frost, A. D. (2008). Cancer incidence in patients with schizophrenia and their first-degree relatives – a meta-analysis. *Acta Psychiatrica Scandinavica, 117*, 323–336.

Danielsen, E. R., & Henriksen, O. (1994). Absolute quantitative proton NMR spectroscopy based on the amplitude of the local water suppression pulse. Quantification of brain water and metabolites. *NMR in Biomedicine, 7*, 311–318.

Dickman, D. K., & Davis, G. W. (2009). The schizophrenia susceptibility gene dysbindin controls synaptic homeostasis. *Science, 326*, 1127–1130.

Elster, C., Schubert, F., Link, A., Walzel, M., Seifert, F., & Rinneberg, H. (2005). Quantitative magnetic resonance spectroscopy: Semi-parametric modeling and determination of uncertainties. *Magnetic Resonance in Medicine, 53*, 1288–1296.

Emamian, E. S., Hall, D., Birnbaum, M. J., Karayiorgou, M., & Gogos, J. A. (2004). Convergent evidence for impaired AKT1-GSK3B signaling in schizophrenia. *Nature Genetics, 36*, 131–137.

Felice, L. J., Felice, J. D., & Kissinger, P. T. (1978). Determination of catecholamines in rat brain parts by reverse-phase ion-pair liquid chromatography. *Journal of Neurochemistry, 31*, 1461–1465.

Gallinat, J., Götz, T., Kalus, P., Bajbouj, M., Sander, T., & Winterer, G. (2007). Genetic variations of the NR3A subunit of the NMDA receptor modulate prefrontal cerebral activity in humans. *Journal of Cognitive Neuroscience, 19*, 59–68.

Gallinat, J., Schubert, F., Brühl, R., Hellweg, R., Klär, A. A., Kehrer, C., ... Lang, U. E. (2010). Met carriers of BDNF Val66Met genotype show increased N-acetylaspartate concentration in the anterior cingulate cortex. *NeuroImage, 49*, 767–771.

Gould, T. D., & Manji, H. K. (2005). Glycogen synthase kinase-3: A putative molecular target for lithium mimetic drugs. *Neuropsychopharmacology, 30*, 1223–1237.

Ikeda, M., Iwata, N., Suzuki, T., Kitajima, T., Yamanouchi, Y., Kinoshita, Y., & Ozaki, N. (2004). Association of AKT1 with schizophrenia confirmed in a Japanese population. *Biological Psychiatry, 56*, 698–700.

Ikeda, Y., Yahata, N., Ito, I., Nagano, M., Toyota, T., Yoshikawa, T., ... Suzuki, H. (2008). Low serum levels of brain-derived neurotrophic factor and epidermal growth factor in patients with chronic schizophrenia. *Schizophrenia Research, 101*, 58–66.

Jagannathan, K., Calhoun, V. D., Gelernter, J., Stevens, M. C., Liu, J., Bolognani, F., ... Pearlson, G. D. (2010). Genetic associations of brain structural networks in schizophrenia: A preliminary study. *Biological Psychiatry, 68*, 657–666.

Jeon, Y. W., & Polich, J. (2003). Meta-analysis of P300 and schizophrenia: Patients, paradigms, and practical implications. *Psychophysiology, 40*, 684–701.

Kalkman, H. O. (2006). The role of phosphoinositide 3-kinase-protein kinase B pathway in schizophrenia. *Pharmacology & Therapeutics, 110*, 117–134.

Kim, J. I., Lee, H. R., Sim, S. E., Beak, J., Yu, N. K., Choi, J. H., ... Kaang, B. K. (2011). PI3Kγ is required for NMDA receptor-dependent long-term depression and behavioral flexibility. *Nature Neuroscience, 14*, 1447–1454.

Klein, P. S., & Melton, D. A. (1996). A molecular mechanism for the effect of lithium on development. *Proceedings of the National Academy of Science of the United States of America, 93*, 8455–8459.

Kreis, R., Ernst, T., & Ross, B. D. (1993). Development of the human brain: In vivo quantification of metabolite and water content with proton magnetic resonance spectroscopy. *Magnetic Resonance in Medicine, 30*, 424–437.

Kumar, V., Zhang, M., Swank, M. W., Kunz, J., & Wu, G. (2005). Regulation of dendritic morphogenesis by Ras-PI3K-AktmTOR and Ras-MAPK signalling pathways. *The Journal of Neuroscience, 25*, 11288–11299.

Lang, F., Böhmer, C., Palmada, M., Seebohm, G., Strutz-Seebohm, N., & Vallon, C. (2006). (Patho)physiological significance of the serum- and glucocorticoid-inducible kinase isoforms. *Physiological Reviews, 86*, 1151–1178.

Lang, U. E., Puls, I., Müller, D. J., Strutz-Seebohm, N., & Gallinat, J. (2007). Molecular mechanisms of schizophrenia. *Cellular Physiology and Biochemistry, 20*, 687–702.

Lawlor, M. A., Mora, A., Ashby, P. R., Williams, M. R., Murray-Tait, V., Malone, L., ... Alessi, D. R. (2002). Essential role of PDK1 in regulating cell size and development in mice. *EMBO Journal, 21*, 3728–3738.

Lee, A. H., Lange, C., Ricken, R., Hellweg, R., & Lang, U. E. (2011). Reduced brain-derived neurotrophic factor serum concentrations in acute schizophrenic patients increase during antipsychotic treatment. *Journal of Clinical Psychopharmacology, 31*, 334–336.

Lu, X. H., & Dwyer, D. S. (2005). Second-generation antipsychotic drugs, olanzapine, quetiapine, and clozapine enhance neurite outgrowth in PC12 cells via PI3K/AKT, ERK, and pertussis toxin-sensitive pathways. *Journal of Molecular Neuroscience, 27*, 43–64.

Martin-Pena, A., Acebes, A., Rodriguez, J., Sorribes, A., de Polavieja, G. G., Fernandez-Funez, P., & Ferrus, A. (2006). Age-independent synaptogenesis by phosphoinositide 3 kinase. *The Journal of Neuroscience, 26*, 10199–10208.

Miller, S. A., Dykes, D. D., & Polesky, H. F. (1988). A simple salting out procedure for extracting DNA from human nucleated cells. *Nucleic Acids Research, 16*, 1215.

Mora, A., Komander, D., van Aalten, D. M., & Alessi, D. R. (2004). PDK1, the master regulator of AGC kinase signal transduction. *Seminars in Cell and Developmental Biology, 15*, 161–170.

Nicodemus, K. K., Law, A. J., Radulescu, E., Luna, A., Kolachana, B., Vakkalanka, R., ... Weinberger, D. R. (2010). Biological validation of increased schizophrenia risk with NRG1, ERBB4, and AKT1 epistasis via functional neuroimaging in healthy controls. *Archives of General Psychiatry, 67*, 991–1001.

Peltier, J., O'Neill, A., & Schaffer, D. V. (2007). PI3K/Akt and CREB regulate adult neural hippocampal progenitor proliferation and differentiation. *Developmental Neurobiology, 67*, 1348–1361.

Piepponen, T. P., & Skujins, A. (2001). Rapid and sensitive step gradient assays of glutamate, glycine, taurine and gammaaminobutyric acid by high-performance liquid chromatography-fluorescence detection with o-phthalaldehydemercaptoethanol derivatization with an emphasis on microdialysis samples. *J. Chromatogr. B. Biomed. Sci. Appl., 757*, 277–283.

Sandu, C., Artunc, F., Palmada, M., Rexhepaj, R., Grahammer, F., Hussain, A., ... Lang, F. (2006). Impaired intestinal NHE3 activity in the PDK1 hypomorphic mouse. *American Journal of Physiology, Gastrointestinal and Liver Physiology, 291*, G868–G876.

Schubert, J., Gallinat, F., Seifert, F., & Rinneberg, H. (2004). Glutamate concentrations in human brain using single voxel proton magnetic resonance spectroscopy at 3 Tesla. *NeuroImage, 21*, 1762–1771.

Schwab, S. G., Hoefgen, B., Hanses, C., Hassenbach, M. B., Albus, M., Lerer, B., ... Wildenauer, D. B. (2005). Further evidence for association of variants in the AKT1 gene with schizophrenia in a sample of European sib-pair families. *Biological Psychiatry, 58*, 446–450.

Shaw, M., Cohen, P., & Alessi, D. R. (1997). Further evidence that the inhibition of glycogen synthase kinase-3beta by IGF-1 is mediated by PDK1/PKB-induced phosphorylation of Ser-9 and not by dephosphorylation of Tyr-216. *F.E.B.S. Letters, 416*, 307–311.

Sheehan, D. V., Lecrubier, Y., Sheehan, K. H., Amorim, P., Janavs, J., Weiller, E., ... Dunbar, G. C. (1998). The Mini-International Neuropsychiatric Interview (M.I.N.I.): The development and validation of a structured diagnostic psychiatric interview for DSM-IV and ICD-10. *Journal of Clinical Psychiatry, 59*, 22–33.

Silvestri, S., Seeman, M. V., Negrete, J. C., Houle, S., Shammi, C. M., Remington, G. J., … Seeman, P. (2000). Increased dopamine D2 receptor binding after long-term treatment with antipsychotics in humans: A clinical PET study. *Psychopharmacology (Berl), 152*, 174–180.

Sperk, G. (1982). Simultaneous determination of serotonin, 5-hydroxindoleacetic acid, 3, 4-dihydroxyphenylacetic acid and homovanillic acid by high performance liquid chromatography with electrochemical detection. *Journal of Neurochemistry, 38*, 840–843.

Sperk, G., Berger, M., Hörtnagl, H., & Hornykiewicz, O. (1981). Kainic acid-induced changes of serotonin and dopamine metabolism in the striatum and substantia nigra of the rat. *European Journal of Pharmacology, 74*, 279–286.

Spitzer, R. L., Williams, J. B., Gibbon, M., & First, M. B. (1992). The Structured Clinical Interview for DSM-III-R (SCID) I: History, rationale, and description. *Archives of General Psychiatry, 49*, 624–629.

van Elst, L. T., Valerius, G., Büchert, M., Thiel, T., Rüsch, N., Bubl, E., … Olbrich, H. M. (2005). Increased prefrontal and hippocampal glutamate concentration in schizophrenia: Evidence from a magnetic resonance spectroscopy study. *Biological Psychiatry, 58*, 724–730.

Vanhaesebroeck, B., & Alessi, D. R. (2000). The PI3KPDK1 connection: More than just a road to PKB. *Biochemical Journal, 346*, 561–576.

Venkatasubramanian, G., Chittiprol, S., Neelakantachar, N., Shetty, T., & Gangadhar, B. N. (2010). Effect of antipsychotic treatment on Insulin-like Growth Factor-1 and cortisol in schizophrenia: A longitudinal study. *Schizophrenia Research, 119*, 131–137.

Waters, F. (2009). Electrophysiological brain activity and antisaccade performance in schizophrenia patients with first-rank (passivity) symptoms. *Psychiatry Research, 170*, 140–149.

Wirth, C., Schubert, F., Lautenschlager, M., Bruhl, R., Klar, A., Majic, T., … Gallinat, J. (2011). DTNBP1 (Dysbindin) Gene Variants: In vivo evidence for effects on hippocampal glutamate status. *Current Pharmaceutical Biotechnology.*

Wüstenberg, T., Begemann, M., Bartels, C., Gefeller, O., Stawicki, S., Hinze-Selch, D., … Ehrenreich, H. (2011). Recombinant human erythropoietin delays loss of gray matter in chronic schizophrenia. *Molecular Psychiatry, 16*, 26–36.

Wyatt, A., Hussain, A., Amann, K., Klingel, K., Kandolf, R., Artunc, F., … Lang, F. (2006). DOCA-induced phosphorylation of glycogen synthase kinase 3beta. *Cellular Physiology Biochemistry, 17*, 137–144.

Undine E. Lang

Department of Psychiatry
University Psychiatric Clinics (UPK)
Wilhelm Klein-Str. 27
4012 Basel
Switzerland
Tel. +41325-5200
Fax +41-61-3255518
E-mail undine.lang@upkbs.ch

Original Article

Subtle Impact of Akt1 and Akt3 on Exploratory Behavior in Gene Targeted Mice

Christina Leibrock,[1] Michael Hierlmeier,[1] Undine E. Lang,[2] and Florian Lang[1]

[1]Department of Physiology I, University of Tuebingen, Germany,
[2]Department of Psychiatry, University of Basel, Switzerland

Abstract. The present study explored the impact of Akt1 and Akt3 on behavior. Akt1 (*akt1*$^{-/-}$) and Akt3 (*akt3*$^{-/-}$) knockout mice were compared to wild type (*wt*) mice. The *akt1*$^{-/-}$ mice, *akt3*$^{-/-}$ mice, and *wt* mice were similar in most parameters of the open-field test. However, the distance traveled in the center area was slightly but significantly less in *akt3*$^{-/-}$ mice than in *wt* mice. In the light/dark transition test *akt1*$^{-/-}$ mice had significantly lower values than *wt* mice and *akt3*$^{-/-}$ mice for distance traveled, number of rearings, rearing time in the light area, as well as time spent and distance traveled in the entrance area. They were significantly different from *akt3*$^{-/-}$ mice in the distance traveled, visits, number of rearings, rearing time in the light area, as well as time spent, distance traveled, number of rearings, and rearing time in the entrance area. In the O-maze the time spent, and the visits to open arms, as well as the number of protected and unprotected headdips were significantly less in *akt1*$^{-/-}$ mice than in *wt* mice, whereas the time spent in closed arms was significantly more in *akt1*$^{-/-}$ mice than in *wt* mice. Protected and unprotected headdips were significantly less in *akt3*$^{-/-}$ mice than in *wt* mice. In closed area, *akt3*$^{-/-}$ mice traveled a significantly larger distance at larger average speed than *akt1*$^{-/-}$ mice. No differences were observed between *akt1*$^{-/-}$ mice, *akt3*$^{-/-}$ mice and *wt*-type mice in the time of floating during the forced swimming test. In conclusion, *akt1*$^{-/-}$ mice and less so *akt3*$^{-/}$ mice display subtle changes in behavior.

Keywords: open-field test, light/dark transition test, O-maze, forced swimming test

Phosphatidylinositide-3 (PI3) kinase-dependent signaling contributes to the cerebral effect of brain-derived neurotrophic factor (BDNF; Wang et al., 1999; Yuan & Yankner, 2000), which in turn participates in the regulation of neuronal plasticity, mood, and memory formation (Michalski & Fahnestock, 2003; Mizuno et al., 2003). Deranged BDNF-dependent regulation may lead to several neuropsychiatric disorders including schizophrenia (Fan & Sklar, 2008; Kuipers & Bramham, 2006; Lang, Hellweg, & Gallinat, 2004, 2005; Lang, Hellweg, Kalus, et al., 2005; Lang, Puls, Muller, Strutz-Seebohm, & Gallinat, 2007; Weickert et al., 2003), depression (Tsai, 2004), and Alzheimer's disease (Michalski & Fahnestock, 2003). Conversely, several psychiatric treatments including antidepressant, neuroleptic, and electroconvulsive therapy are followed by alterations of BDNF concentrations (Meredith, Switzer, & Napier, 2004; Russo-Neustadt, 2003).

Signaling dependent on PI3 kinase includes phosphoinositide-dependent kinase PDK1 and PDK2, which activate the protein kinase B (PKB/Akt) isoforms Ak1, Akt2, and Akt3, as well as the serum and glucocorticoid-inducible kinase isoforms SGK1, SGK2, and SGK3 (Biondi, Kieloch, Currie, Deak, & Alessi, 2001; Chen et al., 2014; Hidalgo et al., 2014; Jia et al., 2014; Kobayashi & Cohen, 1999; Lan, Qi, & Du, 2014; Park et al., 1999; Qi & Zhang, 2014; Qiu et al., 2014; Shieh, Tsai, Tsou, & Wu, 2014; Tsuchiya ct al., 2014; Xiao et al., 2014; Xie et al., 2014; Yu et al., 2014; Zhang, Qian, & Li, 2014; Zhang, Quo, et al., 2014).

Beyond its role in BDNF signaling PI3 K-Akt signaling contributes to cerebral effects of insulin and erythropoietin (Ehrenreich et al., 2004; Elliott, Atlas, Lange, & Ginzburg, 2005; Kalkman, 2006), estrogen (Florian, Lu, Angle, & Magder, 2004) as well as thyroid hormones (Cao, Kambe, Moeller, Refetoff, & Seo, 2005; Cao, Kambe, Yamauchi, & Seo 2009). Moreover, PI3 K-Akt signaling is involved in the therapeutic effects of several drugs including lithium, valproate, olanzapine as well as clozapine on bipolar disorder as well as schizophrenia (Aubry, Schwald, Ballmann, & Karege, 2009; Gould & Manji, 2005; Klein & Melton, 1996; Lu & Dwyer, 2005; Shin et al., 2006) and participates in the sensitization to cocaine (Zhang et al., 2006).

Activated PKB/Akt isoforms phosphorylate and thus inhibit glycogen synthase 3 GSK3 (Cross, Radda, & Clarke, 1995; Shaw, Cohen, & Alessi, 1997). Disruption of Akt-dependent GSK3 phosphorylation (McManus et al., 2005) counteracts anxiety and depression in mice (Ackermann, Kempe, Lang, & Lang, 2010). Conversely, partial lack of phosphoinositide-dependent Akt activating kinase PDK1 (Lawlor et al., 2002) increases anxiety (Ackermann et al., 2008). Akt isoforms further phosphorylate and thus activate phosphatidylinositol-3-phosphate-5-kinase PIKfyve (Berwick et al., 2004), a powerful regulator

DOI: 10.1027/2151-2604/a000218

of excitatory amino acid transporters (Alesutan et al., 2010; Gehring et al., 2009).

Lack of Akt2 leads to enhanced anxiety and depressive behavior in mice (Leibrock et al., 2013). Little is known, however, about the impact of the other two Akt isoforms on behavior. The present study thus aimed to define the role of the isoforms Akt1 and Akt3. To this end, behavioral studies have been performed in Akt1 knockout ($akt1^{-/-}$) mice, Akt3 knockout ($akt3^{-/-}$) mice, and corresponding wild type (*wt*) mice.

Materials and Methods

Animals

The generation, properties, and genotyping of Akt1 or Akt3-deficient mice were described earlier (Cho, Thorvaldsen, Chu, Feng, & Birnbaum, 2001; Easton et al., 2005). Sex and age-matched mice with age more than 2 months were used for the experiments. All animal experiments were conducted according to the German law for the care and use of laboratory animals and were approved by local authorities. For the present study 9 Akt1 knockout mice ($akt1^{-/-}$), 17 Akt3 knockout mice ($akt3^{-/-}$), and 17 wild type littermates (*wt*) were used in two sets of experiments. The age at the beginning of the tests was 12 ± 1 weeks.

Housing and Handling

Mice were bred and housed at Tuebingen. Standard mouse chow, water, and nesting material were available ad libitum. The animals were maintained at a 12:12 hr inverted cycle with lights on between 8 p.m. and 8 a.m. Behavioral testing occurred between 8 a.m. and 8 p.m. Only one type of experiment was done on the same day and the cages were brought to the test room at least 30 min before each experiment and dry surfaces of apparatus were thoroughly cleaned with 70% ethanol before releasing the animal. Experiments extended over a total of 2 weeks for each set and were done in the following order: open-field, light/dark transition test, elevated O-maze, and forced swimming test.

Video Tracking and Illumination

For data acquisition animals were video tracked by the camera 302050-SWE-KIT-2-CAM at a resolution of 0.62 to 0.72 pixel (TSE Systems, Bad Homburg, Germany, www.TSE-Systems.com). Raw data were transferred to Excel for further analysis. Experiments were performed with diffuse indirect room light produced by dimmable bulbs, adjusted to yield less than 30 lux in the center of the experimental arena. The only exception was the light/dark transition test where full room light was switched on to obtain approximately 500 lux in the lit chamber.

Open Field

Procedure

The quadratic open-field arena had a side length of 50 cm and 40 cm high sidewalls. A metallic frame generated a photoelectric barrier within the arena allowing the registration of rearing behavior (vertical activity). For further evaluation a border with 10 cm to the walls was considered dividing the open-field arena in a center and a border area. Each subject was released in the same corner and observed for 30 min.

Parameters

Assessed were global distance and speed as well as distance and time spent in the different regions. Further, the number of crosses over the lines of the virtual grid drawn on the arena surface was detected (horizontal activity). The rearing frame allowed to monitor the number of rearings and the rearing time in the center and the border area (vertical activity).

Light/Dark Transition Test

Procedure

A black acryl box (40 cm high) was inserted into the open-field arena, which covered 33% of the surface area. An aperture of 10 cm length and 11 cm height with rounded down corners led from the lighted arena to the dark box. The experiment was performed under direct room light. Each subject was released in the same corner of the illuminated compartment and observed for 10 min.

Parameters

We recorded the number of visits and the time spent in the illuminated area. As measures of activity while the subject was in the lit chamber we calculated the total distance moved, the number of rearings, and the total rearing time. The entrance area was studied separately. Recorded were time and distance in the entrance area as well as number or rearings and rearing time. The rearing behavior was also monitored in the hidden area.

O-Maze

Procedure

A 5.5 cm wide annular runway was constructed using gray plastic. It had an outer diameter of 46 cm and was located 40 cm above the floor (Konig et al., 1996; Shepherd, Grewal, Fletcher, Bill, & Dourish, 1994). The runway

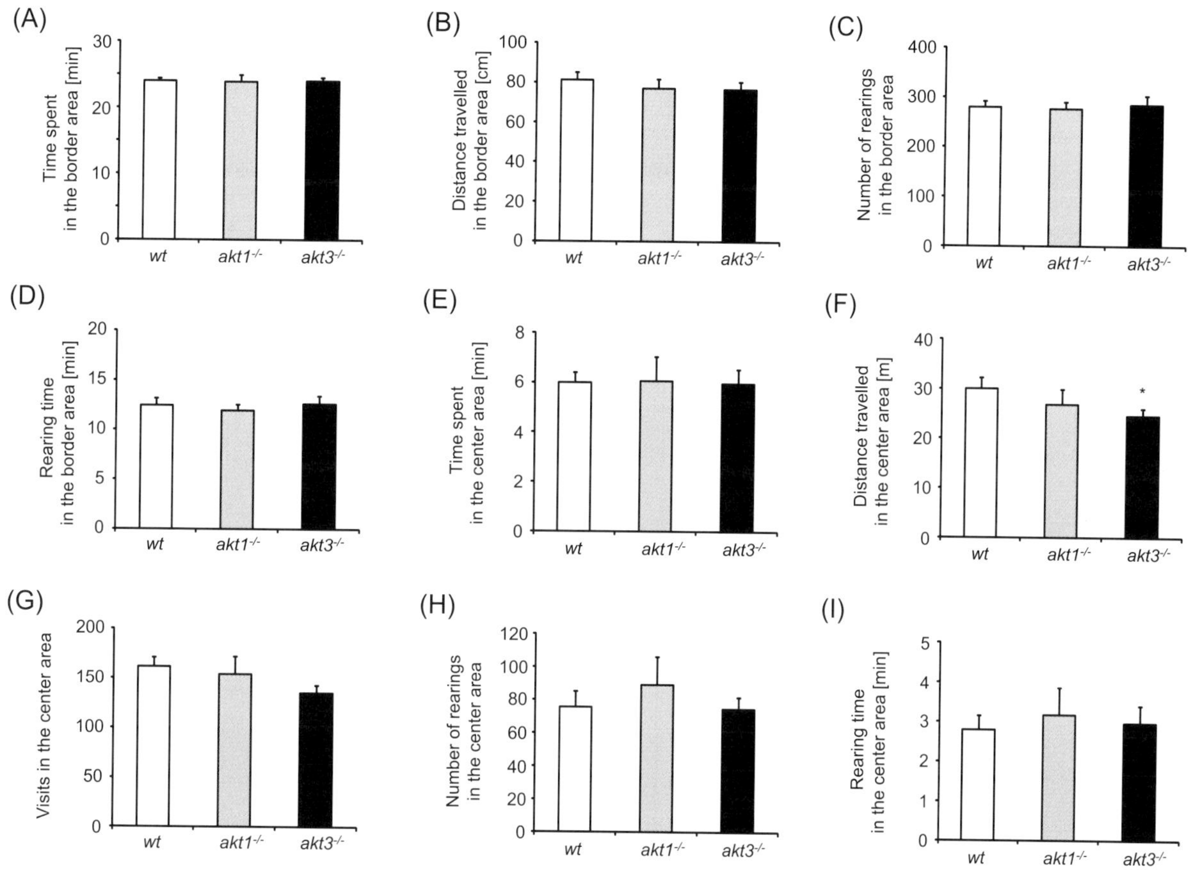

Figure 1. Behavior in open-field test. Arithmetic means ± SEM (n = 17 *wt*, 9 $akt1^{-/-}$, 17 $akt3^{-/-}$) of (A) time spent in the border area of the open field arena, (B) distance traveled in the border area, (C) number of rearings in the border area, (D) rearing time in the border area, (E) time spent in the center area, (F) distance traveled in the center area, (G) visits in the center area, (H) number of rearings in the center area, (I) rearing time in the center area of wild type mice (*wt*, white bars), and of gene targeted mice lacking Akt1 ($akt1^{-/-}$, gray bars) or Akt3 ($akt3^{-/-}$, black bars). *($p < .05$) indicates statistically significant differences from wild type mice.

was divided into four equal-sized sectors, each of them covering 90° of the circle. Two opposing 90° sectors were protected by 11 cm high inner and outer walls and defined as closed areas, while the remaining two open sectors had a border of 5 mm. Animals were released in one of the closed sectors and observed for 10 min. Thereby the mice were not only confronted with a new environment, but also with height. After an acclimatization period mice usually advance onto an unprotected segment of the runway and dip their heads to explore the cliff. This behavior was classified as protected headdip when the body was still in the protected zone. When the protected zone was left completely the exploration of the height was classified as unprotected headdip.

Parameters

Assessed were the numbers of protected and unprotected headdips, time and covered distance in protected and unprotected zones, time spent in the originally closed arm, total distance traveled, and the number of transitions between the areas.

Forced Swimming Test

In the forced swimming test, mice were placed in a container filled with water of temperatures between 24 and 26° C. The diameter of the container was 20 cm. The mouse was placed in the water without being able to touch the ground. Mice were observed during 6 min and the time they spent without movement, called floating, was recorded (Leibrock et al., 2013).

Statistics

For the comparison of the test results of the groups, Student's t-test was used. Only results with $p < .05$ were considered significant.

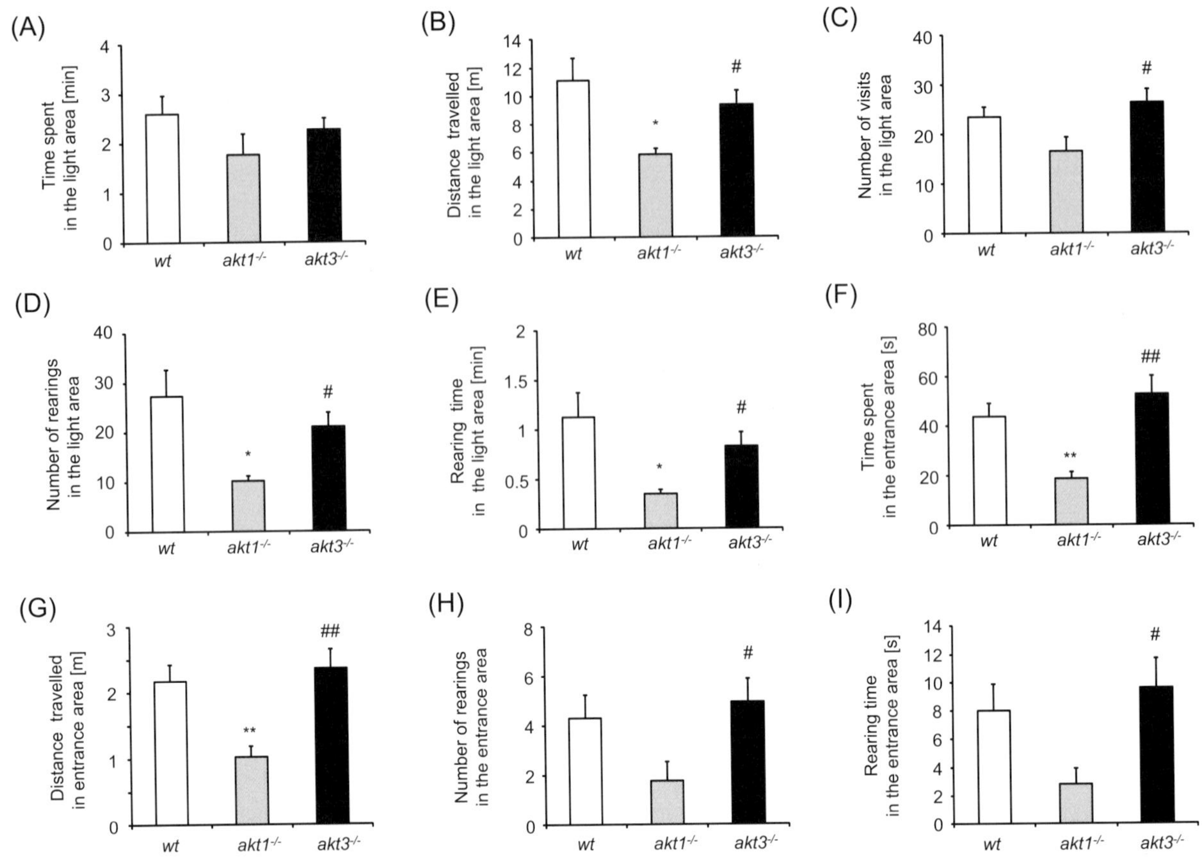

Figure 2. Behavior in light/dark transition test. Arithmetic means ± SEM (n = 17 *wt*, 9 $akt1^{-/-}$, 17 $akt3^{-/-}$) of (A) time spent in the light area, (B) distance traveled in the light area, (C) visits in the light area, (D) number of rearings in the light area, (E) rearing time in the light area, (F) time spent in the entrance area, (G) distance traveled in the entrance area, (H) number of rearings in the entrance area, (I) rearing time in the entrance area of wild type mice (*wt*, white bars), and of gene targeted mice lacking Akt1 ($akt1^{-/-}$, gray bars) or Akt3 ($akt3^{-/-}$, black bars). *($p < .05$), **($p < .01$) indicate statistically significant differences from wild type mice. $^{\#}(p < .05)$, $^{\#\#}(p < .01)$ indicate statistically significant differences from $akt1^{-/-}$ mice.

Results

In order to disclose a putative role of the Akt isoforms Akt1 or Akt3 in the regulation of exploratory behavior, gene targeted mice lacking Akt1 ($akt1^{-/-}$) or Akt3 ($akt3^{-/-}$) were compared to wild type mice (*wt*). Neither the $akt1^{-/-}$ mice nor the $akt3^{-/-}$ mice showed obvious differences of gross behavior to *wt* mice. In order to assess exploratory behavior, the mice were subjected to three forced exploration tests, that is, Open-Field, Light/Dark Transition Test, and elevated O-maze. In those tests the animals were exposed to an entirely new environment.

As illustrated in Figure 1, no significant differences were observed between $akt1^{-/-}$ mice or $akt3^{-/-}$ mice and *wt* mice in most of the parameters obtained with the Open-Field test, that is, time spent in the border area of the Open-Field arena (Figure 1A), distance traveled in the border area (Figure 1B), number of rearings in the border area (Figure 1C), rearing time in the border area (Figure 1D), time spent in the center area (Figure 1E), visits in the center area (Figure 1G), number of rearings in the center area (Figure 1H), and rearing time in the center area (Figure 1I). Moreover, there was no significant difference between the genotypes in global distance traveled (not shown) and average speed (not shown). The distance traveled in the center area tended to be less in $akt1^{-/-}$ mice and was slightly but significantly less in $akt3^{-/-}$ mice (Figure 1F).

The results of the Light/Dark Transition Test are summarized in Figures 2 and 3. As illustrated in Figure 2, $akt1^{-/-}$ mice had lower values than *wt* mice and $akt3^{-/-}$ for each of the parameters obtained, reaching statistical significance versus *wt* mice for distance traveled in the light area (Figure 2B), number of rearings in the light area (Figure 2D), rearing time in the light area (Figure 2E), time spent in the entrance area (Figure 2F), and distance traveled in the entrance area (Figure 2G). The values of $akt1^{-/-}$ mice were statistically significant from those of $akt3^{-/-}$ mice in the distance traveled in the light area (Figure 2B), visits in the light area (Figure 2C), number of rearings in the light area (Figure 2D), rearing time in the light area (Figure 2E),

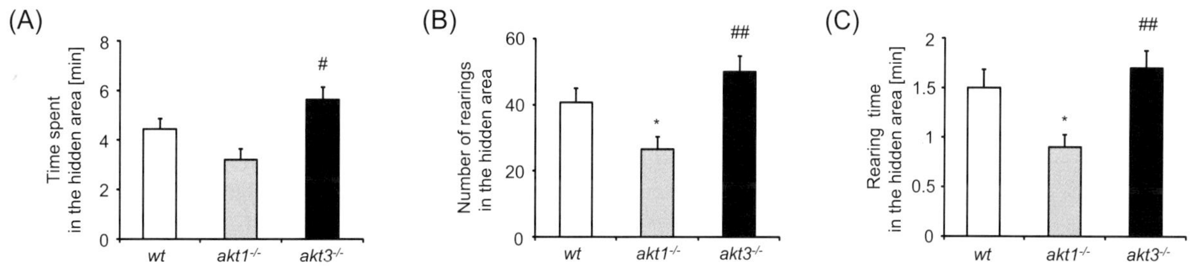

Figure 3. Preference of hidden area in light/dark transition test. Arithmetic means ± SEM (n = 17 *wt*, 9 *akt1*$^{-/-}$, 17 *akt3*$^{-/-}$) of (A) time spent in the hidden area, (B) number of rearings in the hidden area, (C) rearing time in the hidden area of wild type mice (*wt*, white bars), and of gene targeted mice lacking Akt1 (*akt1*$^{-/-}$, gray bars) or Akt3 (*akt3*$^{-/-}$, black bars). *($p < .05$) indicates statistically significant differences from wild type mice. $^{\#}$($p < .05$), $^{\#\#}$($p < .01$) indicate statistically significant differences from *akt1*$^{-/-}$ mice.

time spent in the entrance area (Figure 2F), distance traveled in the entrance area (Figure 2G), number of rearings in the entrance area (Figure 2H), and rearing time in the entrance area (Figure 2I). As illustrated in Figure 3, the *akt1*$^{-/-}$ mice spent less time in the hidden area (Figure 3A), had lower numbers of rearings in the hidden area (Figure 3B), and spent less time for rearing in the hidden area (Figure 3C) than the *wt* mice, differences reaching statistical significance for numbers and time of rearing in hidden area. The *akt1*$^{-/-}$ mice spent significantly less time in

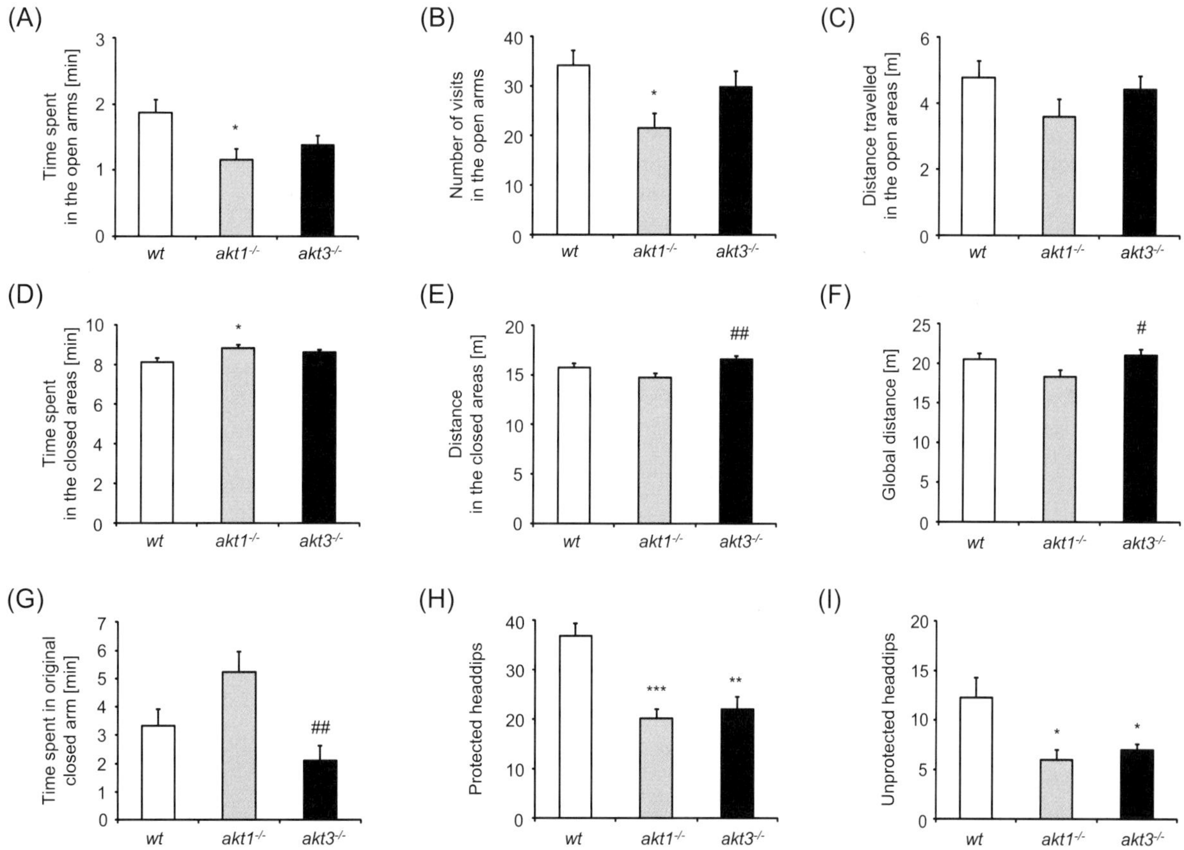

Figure 4. Behavior in O-Maze. Arithmetic means ± SEM (n = 17 *wt*, 9 *akt1*$^{-/-}$, 17 *akt3*$^{-/-}$) of (A) time spent in the open arms, (B) visits in the open arms, (C) distance traveled in the open arms, (D) time spent in the closed arms, (E) distance traveled in the closed arms, (F) global distance traveled, (G) time spent in original closed arm, (H) protected headdips, (I) unprotected headdips of wild type mice (*wt*, white bars), and of gene targeted mice lacking Akt1 (*akt1*$^{-/-}$, gray bars) or Akt3 (*akt3*$^{-/-}$, black bars). *($p < .05$); **($p < .01$). ***($p < .001$) indicate statistically significant differences from wild type mice. $^{\#}$($p < .05$), $^{\#\#}$($p < .01$) indicate statistically significant differences from *akt1*$^{-/-}$ mice.

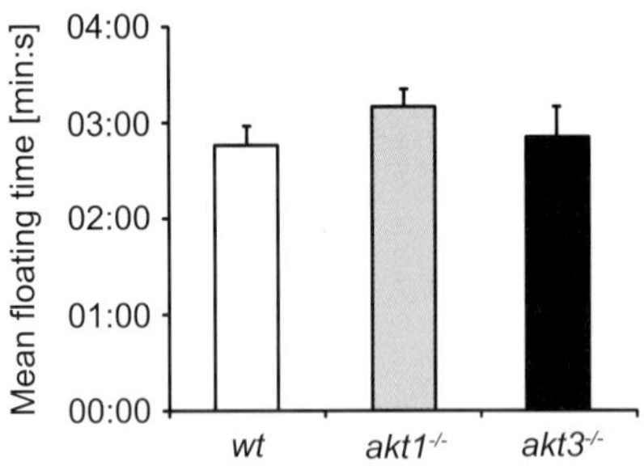

Figure 5. Forced swimming test. Arithmetic means ± SEM (n = 17 *wt*, 9 *akt1*$^{-/-}$, 17 *akt3*$^{-/-}$) of floating time of wild type mice (*wt*, white bars) and of gene targeted mice lacking Akt1 (*akt1*$^{-/-}$, gray bars) or Akt3 (*akt3*$^{-/-}$, black bars).

the hidden area (Figure 3A), had significantly less rearings in the hidden area (Figure 3B), and spent significantly less time for rearing in the hidden area (Figure 3C) than the *akt3*$^{-/-}$ mice. The respective values of *akt3*$^{-/-}$ mice tended to be higher than those in *wt* mice, a difference, however, not reaching statistical significance (Figures 3A–C).

In the O-Maze (Figure 4) the time spent in the open arms (Figure 4A), the number of visits in the open arms (Figure 4B), the number of protected headdips (Figure 4H), and the number of unprotected headdips (Figure 4I) were all significantly less in *akt1*$^{-/-}$ mice than in *wt* mice, whereas the time spent in the closed arms (Figure 4D) was significantly larger in *akt1*$^{-/-}$ mice than in *wt* mice. The number of protected headdips (Figure 4H) and the number of unprotected headdips (Figure 4I) were as well significantly smaller in *akt3*$^{-/-}$ mice than in *wt* mice. The *akt3*$^{-/-}$ mice did not significantly differ from *wt* mice in the other parameters but traveled a significantly larger distance in the closed area (Figure 4E) and traveled a significantly larger global distance (Figure 4F), and at a significantly larger average speed (Figure 4G) than the *akt1*$^{-/-}$ mice.

No significant differences were observed between *akt1*$^{-/-}$ mice, *akt3*$^{-/-}$ mice, and *wt* type mice in the time of floating during the forced swimming test (Figure 5).

Discussion

The present observations revealed only few, subtle differences between *akt3*$^{-/-}$ mice and *wt*$^{-}$ mice. In the open-field test, only the distance traveled in the center area was slightly but significantly less in *akt3*$^{-/-}$ mice than in *wt* mice. In the light/dark transition test the number of protected headdips and the number of unprotected headdips were significantly smaller in *akt3*$^{-/-}$ mice than in *wt* mice. In none of the other measured parameters did the *akt3*$^{-/-}$ mice significantly differ from *wt* mice.

The study disclosed several differences between *akt1*$^{-/-}$ and *wt* and/or *akt3*$^{-/-}$ mice. In the light/dark transition test *akt1*$^{-/-}$ mice had significantly lower values than *wt* mice and/or *akt3*$^{-/-}$ mice for distance traveled in the light area, number of rearings in the light area, rearing time in the light area, time spent in the entrance area, distance traveled in the entrance area, visits in the light area, number of rearings in the entrance area, and rearing time in the entrance area. In the O-maze the time spent in the open arms, the number of visits in the open arms, the number of protected headdips, and the number of unprotected headdips were all significantly less in *akt1*$^{-/-}$ mice than in *wt* mice, whereas the time spent in the closed arms was significantly larger in *akt1*$^{-/-}$ mice than in *wt* mice. The *akt1*$^{-/-}$ mice traveled a significantly smaller distance in the closed areas, traveled a significantly smaller global distance, and traveled at significantly smaller average speed than the *akt3*$^{-/-}$ mice.

The behavioral phenotype of *akt1*$^{-/-}$ and *akt3*$^{-/-}$ mice was less striking than the phenotype of *akt2*$^{-/-}$ mice which displayed enhanced anxiety and depressive behavior with decreased locomotor activity in several environments (Leibrock et al., 2013). Most importantly the forced swimming test did not disclose any significant differences between *akt1*$^{-/-}$ or *akt3*$^{-/-}$ mice and *wt* mice, suggesting that unlike the *akt2*$^{-/-}$ mice (Leibrock et al., 2013), *akt1*$^{-/-}$ or *akt3*$^{-/-}$ mice do not display depressive behavior. However, *akt2*$^{-/-}$ mice did similarly not display a strong phenotype in several anxiety-related behaviors other than increased agoraphobia in the open field (Leibrock et al., 2013).

Taken together, the Akt1 and Akt3 isoforms appear to have a slight but partially significant effect on exploratory behavior. Possibly the Akt and Sgk isoforms are able to partially replace each other thus mitigating the impact on behavior of genetic knockout of a single isoform.

The Akt isoforms are activated by phosphorylation through PI3-K (Biondi et al., 2001; Kobayashi & Cohen, 1999; Park et al., 1999), which contributes to the signaling of BDNF (Mizuno et al., 2003). BDNF contributes in turn to the regulation of depressive behavior in mice and men (Lang et al., 2004; Manji et al., 2003; Russo-Neustadt, 2003). Thus, reduced locomotion of *akt2*$^{-/-}$ mice (Leibrock et al., 2013) and less so of the *akt1*$^{-/-}$ mice could in part reflect disruption of BDNF signaling.

In conclusion, genetic lack of Akt1 and less so lack of Akt3 leads to slight and partially significant decrease of exploratory behavior without significantly influencing depressive behavior. The observations indicate that more than one Akt isform may participate in the shaping of murine behavior.

Acknowledgments

Christina Leibrock and Michael Hierlmeier contributed equally to this paper. This work was supported by the Swiss National Science Foundation and the Deutsche Forschungsgemeinschaft.

References

Ackermann, T. F., Hortnagl, H., Wolfer, D. P., Colacicco, G., Sohr, R., Lang, F., ... Lang, U. E. (2008). Phosphatidylinositide dependent kinase deficiency increases anxiety and decreases GABA and serotonin abundance in the amygdala. *Cellular Physiology and Biochemistry, 22*, 735–744. doi: 10.1159/000185557

Ackermann, T. F., Kempe, D. S., Lang, F., & Lang, U. E. (2010). Hyperactivity and enhanced curiosity of mice expressing PKB/SGK-resistant glycogen synthase kinase-3 (GSK-3). *Cellular Physiology and Biochemistry, 25*, 775–786.

Alesutan, I. S., Ureche, O. N., Laufer, J., Klaus, F., Zurn, A., Lindner, R., . . . Lang, F. (2010). Regulation of the glutamate transporter EAAT4 by PIKfyve. *Cellular Physiology and Biochemistry, 25*, 187–194.

Aubry, J. M., Schwald, M., Ballmann, E., & Karege, F. (2009). Early effects of mood stabilizers on the Akt/GSK-3beta signaling pathway and on cell survival and proliferation. *Psychopharmacology (Berlin), 205*, 419–429.

Berwick, D. C., Dell, G. C., Welsh, G. I., Heesom, K. J., Hers, I., Fletcher, L. M., . . . Tavare, J. M. (2004). Protein kinase B phosphorylation of PIKfyve regulates the trafficking of GLUT4 vesicles. *Journal of Cell Science, 117*, 5985–5993.

Biondi, R. M., Kieloch, A., Currie, R. A., Deak, M., & Alessi, D. R. (2001). The PIF-binding pocket in PDK1 is essential for activation of S6K and SGK, but not PKB. *EMBO Journal, 20*, 4380–4390.

Cao, X., Kambe, F., Moeller, L. C., Refetoff, S., & Seo, H. (2005). Thyroid hormone induces rapid activation of Akt/protein kinase B-mammalian target of rapamycin-p70S6 K cascade through phosphatidylinositol 3-kinase in human fibroblasts. *Molecular Endocrinology, 19*, 102–112.

Cao, X., Kambe, F., Yamauchi, M., & Seo, H. (2009). Thyroid-hormone-dependent activation of the phosphoinositide 3-kinase/Akt cascade requires Src and enhances neuronal survival. *Biochemical Journal, 424*, 201–209.

Chen, W., Zheng, G., Yang, S., Ping, W., Fu, X., Zhang, N., . . . Wang, J. (2014). CYP2J2 and EETs protect against oxidative stress and apoptosis in vivo and in vitro following lung ischemia/reperfusion. *Cellular Physiology and Biochemistry, 33*, 1663–1680. doi: 10.1159/000362950

Cho, H., Thorvaldsen, J. L., Chu, Q., Feng, F., & Birnbaum, M. J. (2001). Akt1/PKBalpha is required for normal growth but dispensable for maintenance of glucose homeostasis in mice. *Journal of Biological Chemistry, 276*, 38349–38352. doi: 10.1074/jbc.C100462200

Cross, H. R., Radda, G. K., & Clarke, K. (1995). The role of Na+/K+ ATPase activity during low flow ischemia in preventing myocardial injury: A 31P, 23Na and 87Rb NMR spectroscopic study. *Magnetic Resonance in Medicine, 34*, 673–685.

Easton, R. M., Cho, H., Roovers, K., Shineman, D. W., Mizrahi, M., Forman, M. S., . . . Birnbaum, M. J. (2005). Role for Akt3/protein kinase Bgamma in attainment of normal brain size. *Molecular Cell Biology, 25*, 1869–1878. doi: 10.1128/MCB.25.5.1869-1878.2005

Ehrenreich, H., Aust, C., Krampe, H., Jahn, H., Jacob, S., Herrmann, M., & Siren, A. L. (2004). Erythropoietin: Novel approaches to neuroprotection in human brain disease. *Metabolic Brain Disease, 19*, 195–206.

Elliott, E., Atlas, R., Lange, A., & Ginzburg, I. (2005). Brain-derived neurotrophic factor induces a rapid dephosphorylation of tau protein through a PI-3 Kinase signalling mechanism. *European Journal of Neuroscience, 22*, 1081–1089.

Fan, J., & Sklar, P. (2008). Genetics of bipolar disorder: Focus on BDNF Val66Met polymorphism. *Novartis Foundation Symposium, 289*, 60–72.

Florian, M., Lu, Y., Angle, M., & Magder, S. (2004). Estrogen induced changes in Akt-dependent activation of endothelial nitric oxide synthase and vasodilation. *Steroids, 69*, 637–645.

Gehring, E. M., Zurn, A., Klaus, F., Laufer, J., Sopjani, M., Lindner, R., . . . Lang, F. (2009). Regulation of the glutamate transporter EAAT2 by PIKfyve. *Cellular Physiology and Biochemistry, 24*, 361–368.

Gould, T. D., & Manji, H. K. (2005). Glycogen synthase kinase-3: A putative molecular target for lithium mimetic drugs. *Neuropsychopharmacology, 30*, 1223–1237.

Hidalgo, M., Marchant, D., Quidu, P., Youcef-Ali, K., Richalet, J. P., Beaudry, M., . . . Launay, T. (2014). Oxygen modulates the glutathione peroxidase activity during the L6 myoblast early differentiation process. *Cellular Physiology and Biochemistry, 33*, 67–77. doi: 10.1159/000356650

Jia, R. Z., Ding, G. C., Gu, C. M., Huang, T., Rui, C., Wang, Y. X., & Lu, Q. (2014). CDX2 enhances HTR-8/SVneo trophoblast cell invasion by altering the expression of matrix metalloproteinases. *Cellular Physiology and Biochemistry, 34*, 628–636. doi: 10.1159/000363028

Kalkman, H. O. (2006). The role of the phosphatidylinositide 3-kinase-protein kinase B pathway in schizophrenia. *Pharmacology & Therapeutics, 110*, 117–134.

Klein, P. S., & Melton, D. A. (1996). A molecular mechanism for the effect of lithium on development. *Proceedings of the National Academy of Sciences of the United States of America, 93*, 8455–8459.

Kobayashi, T., & Cohen, P. (1999). Activation of serum- and glucocorticoid-regulated protein kinase by agonists that activate phosphatidylinositide 3-kinase is mediated by 3-phosphoinositide-dependent protein kinase-1 (PDK1) and PDK2. *Biochemical Journal, 339*, 319–328.

Konig, M., Zimmer, A. M., Steiner, H., Holmes, P. V., Crawley, J. N., Brownstein, M. J., & Zimmer, A. (1996). Pain responses, anxiety and aggression in mice deficient in pre-proenkephalin. *Nature, 383*, 535–538.

Kuipers, S. D., & Bramham, C. R. (2006). Brain-derived neurotrophic factor mechanisms and function in adult synaptic plasticity: New insights and implications for therapy. *Current Opinion in Drug Discovery and Development, 9*, 580–586.

Lan, A., Qi, Y., & Du, J. (2014). Akt2 mediates TGF-beta1-induced epithelial to mesenchymal transition by deactivating GSK3beta/snail signaling pathway in renal tubular epithelial cells. *Cellular Physiology and Biochemistry, 34*, 368–382. doi: 10.1159/000363006

Lang, U. E., Hellweg, R., & Gallinat, J. (2004). BDNF serum concentrations in healthy volunteers are associated with depression-related personality traits. *Neuropsychopharmacology, 29*, 795–798. Retrieved from http://www.ncbi.nlm.nih.gov/pubmed/14735133

Lang, U. E., Hellweg, R., & Gallinat, J. (2005). Association of BDNF serum concentrations with central serotonergic activity: Evidence from auditory signal processing. *Neuropsychopharmacology, 30*, 1148–1153.

Lang, U. E., Hellweg, R., Kalus, P., Bajbouj, M., Lenzen, K. P., Sander, T., . . . Gallinat, J. (2005). Association of a functional BDNF polymorphism and anxiety-related personality traits. *Psychopharmacology (Berlin), 180*, 95–99.

Lang, U. E., Puls, I., Muller, D. J., Strutz-Seebohm, N., & Gallinat, J. (2007). Molecular mechanisms of schizophrenia. *Cellular Physiology and Biochemistry, 20*, 687–702.

Lawlor, M. A., Mora, A., Ashby, P. R., Williams, M. R., Murray-Tait, V., Malone, L., . . . Alessi, D. R. (2002). Essential role of PDK1 in regulating cell size and development in mice. *EMBO Journal, 21*, 3728–3738.

Leibrock, C., Ackermann, T. F., Hierlmeier, M., Lang, F., Borgwardt, S., & Lang, U. E. (2013). Akt2 deficiency is associated with anxiety and depressive behavior in mice. *Cellular Physiology and Biochemistry, 32*, 766–777. doi: 10.1159/000354478

Lu, X. H., & Dwyer, D. S. (2005). Second-generation antipsychotic drugs, olanzapine, quetiapine, and clozapine enhance neurite outgrowth in PC12 cells via PI3 K/AKT, ERK, and pertussis toxin-sensitive pathways. *Journal of Molecular Neuroscience, 27*, 43–64.

Manji, H. K., Quiroz, J. A., Sporn, J., Payne, J. L., Denicoff, K., Gray, A., ... Charney, D. S. (2003). Enhancing neuronal plasticity and cellular resilience to develop novel, improved therapeutics for difficult-to-treat depression. *Biological Psychiatry, 53*, 707–742.

McManus, E. J., Sakamoto, K., Armit, L. J., Ronaldson, L., Shpiro, N., Marquez, R., & Alessi, D. R. (2005). Role that phosphorylation of GSK3 plays in insulin and Wnt signalling defined by knockin analysis. *EMBO Journal, 24*, 1571–1583.

Meredith, G. E., Switzer, R. C. III, & Napier, T. C. (2004). Short-term, D2 receptor blockade induces synaptic degeneration, reduces levels of tyrosine hydroxylase and brain-derived neurotrophic factor, and enhances D2-mediated firing in the ventral pallidum. *Brain Research, 995*, 14–22.

Michalski, B., & Fahnestock, M. (2003). Pro-brain-derived neurotrophic factor is decreased in parietal cortex in Alzheimer's disease. *Molecular Brain Research, 111*, 148–154.

Mizuno, M., Yamada, K., Takei, N., Tran, M. H., He, J., Nakajima, A., ... Nabeshima, T. (2003). Phosphatidylinositol 3-kinase: A molecule mediating BDNF-dependent spatial memory formation. *Molecular Psychiatry, 8*, 217–224.

Park, J., Leong, M. L., Buse, P., Maiyar, A. C., Firestone, G. L., & Hemmings, B. A. (1999). Serum and glucocorticoid-inducible kinase (SGK) is a target of the PI 3-kinase-stimulated signaling pathway. *EMBO Journal, 18*, 3024–3033.

Qi, L., & Zhang, Y. (2014). The microRNA 132 regulates fluid shear stress-induced differentiation in periodontal ligament cells through mTOR signaling pathway. *Cellular Physiology and Biochemistry, 33*, 433–445. doi: 10.1159/000358624

Qiu, C., Xie, Q., Zhang, D., Chen, Q., Hu, J., & Xu, L. (2014). GM-CSF induces cyclin D1 expression and proliferation of endothelial progenitor cells via PI3 K and MAPK signaling. *Cellular Physiology and Biochemistry, 33*, 784–795. doi: 10.1159/000358652

Russo-Neustadt, A. (2003). Brain-derived neurotrophic factor, behavior, and new directions for the treatment of mental disorders. *Seminars in Clinical Neuropsychiatry, 8*, 109–118.

Shaw, M., Cohen, P., & Alessi, D. R. (1997). Further evidence that the inhibition of glycogen synthase kinase-3beta by IGF-1 is mediated by PDK1/PKB-induced phosphorylation of Ser-9 and not by dephosphorylation of Tyr-216. *FEBS Letters, 416*, 307–311.

Shepherd, J. K., Grewal, S. S., Fletcher, A., Bill, D. J., & Dourish, C. T. (1994). Behavioural and pharmacological characterisation of the elevated "zero-maze" as an animal model of anxiety. *Psychopharmacology (Berlin), 116*, 56–64.

Shieh, J. M., Tsai, Y. J., Tsou, C. J., & Wu, W. B. (2014). CXCL1 regulation in human pulmonary epithelial cells by tumor necrosis factor. *Cellular Physiology and Biochemistry, 34*, 1373–1384. doi: 10.1159/000366344

Shin, S. Y., Choi, B. H., Ko, J., Kim, S. H., Kim, Y. S., & Lee, Y. H. (2006). Clozapine, a neuroleptic agent, inhibits Akt by counteracting Ca2+/calmodulin in PTEN-negative U-87MG human glioblastoma cells. *Cell Signaling, 18*, 1876–1886.

Tsai, S. J. (2004). Down-regulation of the Trk-B signal pathway: The possible pathogenesis of major depression. *Medical Hypotheses, 62*, 215–218.

Tsuchiya, A., Kanno, T., Nagaya, H., Shimizu, T., Tanaka, A., & Nishizaki, T. (2014). PTP1B inhibition causes Rac1 activation by enhancing receptor tyrosine kinase signaling. *Cellular Physiology and Biochemistry, 33*, 1097–1105. doi: 10.1159/000358679

Wang, Q., Somwar, R., Bilan, P. J., Liu, Z., Jin, J., Woodgett, J. R., & Klip, A. (1999). Protein kinase B/Akt participates in GLUT4 translocation by insulin in L6 myoblasts. *Molecular Cell Biology, 19*, 4008–4018.

Weickert, C. S., Hyde, T. M., Lipska, B. K., Herman, M. M., Weinberger, D. R., & Kleinman, J. E. (2003). Reduced brain-derived neurotrophic factor in prefrontal cortex of patients with schizophrenia. *Molecular Psychiatry, 8*, 592–610.

Xiao, Y., Qu, C., Ge, W., Wang, B., Wu, J., Xu, L., & Chen, Y. (2014). Depletion of thymosin beta4 promotes the proliferation, migration, and activation of human hepatic stellate cells. *Cellular Physiology and Biochemistry, 34*, 356–367. doi: 10.1159/000363005

Xie, M., Yi, X., Wang, R., Wang, L., He, G., Zhu, M., ... Tang, A. (2014). 14-thienyl methylene matrine (YYJ18), the derivative from matrine, induces apoptosis of human nasopharyngeal carcinoma cells by targeting MAPK and PI3 K/Akt pathways in vitro. *Cellular Physiology and Biochemistry, 33*, 1475–1483. doi: 10.1159/000358712

Yu, W., Shen, T., Liu, B., Wang, S., Li, J., Dai, D., ... He, Q. (2014). Cardiac shock wave therapy attenuates H9c2 myoblast apoptosis by activating the AKT signal pathway. *Cellular Physiology and Biochemistry, 33*, 1293–1303. doi: 10.1159/000358697

Yuan, J., & Yankner, B. A. (2000). Apoptosis in the nervous system. *Nature, 407*, 802–809.

Zhang, H., Guo, M., Chen, J. H., Wang, Z., Du, X. F., Liu, P. X., & Li, W. H. (2014). Osteopontin knockdown inhibits alphav, beta3 integrin-induced cell migration and invasion and promotes apoptosis of breast cancer cells by inducing autophagy and inactivating the PI3 K/Akt/mTOR pathway. *Cellular Physiology and Biochemistry, 33*, 991–1002. doi: 10.1159/000358670

Zhang, W., Qian, C., & Li, S. Q. (2014). Protective effect of SGK1 in rat hippocampal neurons subjected to ischemia reperfusion. *Cellular Physiology and Biochemistry, 34*, 299–312. doi: 10.1159/000363000

Zhang, X., Mi, J., Wetsel, W. C., Davidson, C., Xiong, X., Chen, Q., ... Lee, T. H. (2006). PI3 kinase is involved in cocaine behavioral sensitization and its reversal with brain area specificity. *Biochemical and Biophysical Research Communications, 340*, 1144–1150.

Florian Lang

Department of Physiology
University of Tuebingen
Gmelinstr. 5
72076 Tuebingen
Germany
Tel. +49 1786 241-689
Fax +49 7071 293-073
E-mail florian.lang@uni-tuebingen.de

Original Article

Transgenerational Transmission of Stress Pathology

Contributions of Rodent Models

Margarete Bolten

Child and Adolescent Psychiatric Clinic, University of Basel, Switzerland

Abstract. The impact of the environment early in life on long-term outcomes is well known. Stressful experiences during pre- and postnatal development can modulate the genetic programming of specific brain circuits underlying emotional and cognitive aspects of behavioral adaptation to stressful experiences later in life. Furthermore, there is documented evidence for gene-environment interactions in the context of early-life stress. Identical gene variants can be associated with different phenotypes depending on environmental factors. DNA methylation, an enzymatically-catalyzed modification of the DNA, is the mechanism through which phenotypes are regulated. The dynamics and plasticity of epigenetic mechanisms can have short-term, long-term, or transgenerational consequences. In epigenetic research, rodent models have targeted several behavioral and emotional phenotypes. These models have contributed significantly to our understanding of the environmental regulation of the developmental brain in early life. This review will highlight studies with rats and mice on epigenetic processes in fetal programming of stress-related mental disorders.

Keywords: early-life adversity, Fetal programming, epigenetics, brain development, psychiatric disease

Very early in the life cycle, the brain is particularly sensitive to influences by environmental factors. Hence the idea came up that the pre- or postnatal environment may not only imprint adult health but also diseases. This hypothesis was first proposed by Barker (1993) based on epidemiological observations that a low birth weight increases the risks of a Metabolic Syndrome (cardiovascular disease and type 2 diabetes) later in life. The so-called "Fetal Origins Hypothesis" is accepted by the majority of the scientific community in this field and has successively been extended to other diseases, including functional changes in the brain, which might cause psychiatric disorders. Further research on early life influences also includes peri- and postnatal development; therefore this review uses the term "Early-Life Programming." The research efforts during the past decades have provided evidence suggesting that early-life stress (ELS) may modulate the genetic programming of specific brain circuits underlying emotional and cognitive aspects of behavioral adaptation to stressful experiences later in life, predisposing individuals to the development of psychopathologies (Babenko, Kovalchuk, & Metz, 2015; Barnes & Ozanne, 2011; Branchi & Cirulli, 2014; Champagne, 2013; Kapoor, Petropoulos, & Matthews, 2008). Animal models, especially rodents, have contributed significantly to our understanding of the environmental regulation of the brain. There is a high plasticity in neurobiological pathways regulating stress responsivity, cognition, and breeding behavior during early development that continues into adulthood, suggesting a high sensitivity to environmental cues. This phenomenon is often called "Early-Life Programming" and is associated with an increased risk of disease.

The effects of Early-Life Programming are mediated by two main stress systems, the hypothalamus-pituitary-adrenal (HPA)-axis and the autonomic nervous system (Kapoor et al., 2008; Murgatroyd & Spengler, 2011). Research has shown that ELS produces epigenetic modifications, molecular changes that alter gene expression without altering the underlying DNA sequence, in the HPA axis (Maccari, Krugers, Morley-Fletcher, Szyf, & Brunton, 2014). This includes hormones and receptors that regulate the organism's response and adaptation to stress: the corticotrophin releasing hormone (CRH), cortisol and corticosterone (CORT), and the receptors for circulating adrenal corticoids (Murgatroyd & Spengler, 2012, 2014).

The majority of animal models in studies on pre- and postnatal stress use rodents, and therefore this review relies on this species. Nevertheless, there are also studies with sheep, pigs, or guinea pigs as well as nonhuman primates. Rodents are used so often as models because they are small, easily breed in the laboratory, genetically very homogeneous, and are suitable for many types of experimental manipulations. Furthermore, rats and mice are genetically, biologically, and behaviorally close to human beings.

DOI: 10.1027/2151-2604/a000219

Many symptoms of human beings can be replicated in these species. Their anatomy, physiology, and genetics are well understood and they share many processes and behaviors with human beings, including the stress response, fear, or breeding behavior. For instance, like human babies, newborn rats are dependent on their mothers, they remain in close contact, and early experiences with their mothers shape the behavioral and neurochemical phenotype of the offspring. Furthermore, rat models are used because there are considerable variations in the naturally occurring variations in maternal care (Champagne, Francis, Mar, & Meaney, 2003). The frequency of how often a rat mother licks and grooms her pups is a stable behavioral trait that is normally distributed across dams. This licking and grooming (LG) behavior is a major source of tactile stimulation for the neonatal rat that regulates several physiological systems of the neonate. There is considerable evidence for the sustained effect of maternal care on offspring's behavioral and endocrine responses to stress (Bagot et al., 2012; Champagne, 2013; Pena, Neugut, Calarco, & Champagne, 2014; Sequeira-Cordero, Masis-Calvo, Mora-Gallegos, & Fornaguera-Trias, 2013). LG is associated with the hippocampal development, especially with the concentration of hippocampal glucocorticoid receptors (GR) in the adult rat. These changes in the GRs affect the hypothalamic-pituitary-adrenal (HPA) axis response to stress, learning, and memory.

In conclusion, rodent studies may have the utility in uncovering endophenotypes caused by the ELS. Based on existing evidence from studies with rodents summarized in this review, it is proposed that ELS is one of the most powerful influences on mental health in human beings. Since we know that mental disorders might have gender-specific pathophysiology, special attention is also given the differential effects of ELS on the in female versus male offspring. Putting attention on gender-specific lifetime trajectories of mental disorders is critical for the development of strategies that support healthy development and successful aging.

Early-Life Stress and Its Implications for Brain Development and Behavior

The programming of neuroendocrine, behavioral, or metabolic processes in response to the social or physical environment early in life as an adjustment to anticipated lifelong experiences may be adaptive, permitting an organism to cope with future life conditions (Maccari et al., 2014). However very often, these adaptations could become maladaptive if social and other environmental contexts are altered later in life, increasing the susceptibility of an individual to pathologies such as mental disorders. The following two paragraphs review methods and findings from rodent studies on pre- as well postnatal programming of specific brain circuits underlying emotional and cognitive aspects of behavioral adaptation to stressful experiences later in life. There are some factors, which an impact on the developmental outcome of the ELS exposed offspring. These factors can be protective or risk factors and must be taken into account: the timing (early, mid- or late-gestation), the type (compare Tables 1 and 3), frequency and potency of the stressors, as well as the sex and age of the offspring when outcome phenotypes are measured (e.g., juvenile, adult, or aged).

Studies on Prenatal Stress

Rodent studies use different experimental paradigms to study the impact of prenatal stress (PS): (a) Immobilization (restrained stress), (b) electric shocks, (c) social stress, (d) fetal exposure to glucocorticoids (GC), (e) hypoxia, or (f) dietary manipulations. In Table 1, you find an overview of commonly used paradigms used in studies with rats or mice.

Exposed rodent offspring show (a) enhanced neuroendocrine stress responses, (b) increased levels of anxiety, (c) depressive-like behaviors, (d) sleep behavior, or (e) learning and memory deficits. The underlying mechanisms are very similar in all outcomes: impaired GC negative-feedback control of the hypothalamic-pituitary-adrenal (HPA) axis, altered glutamate neurotransmission, and reduced hippocampal neurogenesis.

HPA-Axis Dysfunction

The effects of PS or prenatally administered synthetic GCs such as dexamethasone (DEX) on the HPA axis in the offspring have been studied extensively. Exposure to high levels of GCs, either caused by PS, or by synthetic GCs administration, induces apoptosis (programmed cell dead) in regions of the rodent brain including the hippocampus, hypothalamus, and cortex (Lu et al., 2013). Furthermore, PS alters basal cortisol levels in the way that rats have higher CORT levels (Bhatnagar, Lee, & Vining, 2005; Maccari et al., 2003; Van den Hove et al., 2014). PS offspring (male and female) exhibit extended and enhanced CORT responses to stress (Koehl et al., 1999; Vallee, Mayo, Maccari, Le Moal, & Simon, 1996; Weinstock, Matlina, Maor, Rosen, & McEwen, 1992; Wilcoxon & Redei, 2007). The extended CORT responses to stress in PS offspring are related to dampened levels of both hippocampal GR and mineralcorticoid receptors (MR), which can be found in the neonate, adolescent, and adult offspring (Belay et al., 2011; Green et al., 2011). Concordantly, the expression of GR and MR mRNA was reduced in the hippocampus in adult PS offspring (Garcia-Caceres et al., 2010; Green et al., 2011; Yu, Lee, Lee, & Son, 2004). These findings indicate an impaired GC negative-feedback control of the HPA axis in PS offspring. The amygdala, part of the limbic system, is involved in the reactivity of the HPA axis to stressors as well as many cognitive, emotional, or social processes, and regulates a variety of behaviors (including aggression, depressive and anxiety behaviors). Morphologically and functionally

Table 1. Models to induce prenatal stress in rodents

Restrained (or Immobilization) Stress Model
The Restrained Stress model is a somewhat milder form of stress induced by immobilization of the pregnant rat. The procedure is highly variable and can differ a lot between research groups. At an extreme end, animals are taped down to immobilize them completely, for a period between 1 and 2 hrs. A much milder form of restraint stress is to place rats in small cages or cylinders that limit their movement. Usually the restraining period lasts between 30 min and 2 hrs once per day. During this time, the rats have no access to food or water, but sufficient oxygen.

Social Stress Model
In the Social Stress model a pregnant rat is repeatedly transferred to a cage with an unfamiliar (and therefore aggressive) lactating rat for 10–30 min/day. The advantage of this model is the high ecological validity, because social distress is the type of stress that pregnant women are likely to experience.

Maternal Dietary Manipulation Model
Maternal dietary manipulation models are very diverse, ranging from undernutrition, over single nutrient restrictions (e.g., low protein) to micronutrient restrictions. Hence the type and severity of the insults caused the nutrient manipulations to vary a lot between models. A general finding is that undernutrition or restriction of specific nutrients promotes an increase in GC in the mother. Furthermore, protein restriction seems to reduce the expression of placental 11β-hydroxysteroid dehydrogenase type 2 (11β-HSD2), a key enzyme which protects the fetus from overexposure to GCs by oxidation into inactive derivates. From this it follows that dietary manipulation acts as a stimulation for the secretion of stress hormones itself and disturbs the inactivation of GC, which leads to an exposure with these hormones.

Noise Pollution Model
In this model stress is induced by an acute or chronic exposure to loud noise that has the potential to stimulate the sympathetic nervous system (Leq $<$ 90 dB) or the HPA axis (Leq $<$ 120 dB). In rats a dose-response relationship of stress hormones under exposure to traffic noise was demonstrated (Okada et al., 1985).

Exposure to synthetic glucocorticoids (GC)
The direct exposure of the fetus with endogenous glucocorticoids (GCs) is another model to study the impact of prenatal stress. GCs are important for fetal growth and tissue development, nevertheless an overexposure with GCs has adverse effects. GCs are highly lipophilic and can easily cross the placenta, but as mentioned above the enzyme 11β-HSD2 inactivates them to cortison. Studies use different synthetic GCs (betamethasone, dexamethasone) in different dosages (0.05–0.5 mg/kg) during different time points in gestation (early, middle, late gestation). Usually GCs are applicated.

alterations in the amygdala interfere therefore with emotional memory processing (Brunton & Russell, 2010). Deficits in emotional, cognitive, or behavioral functioning in rodents may therefore be explained by modifications in the amygdala region (Sampedro-Piquero, Zancada-Menendez, Begega, Rubio, & Arias, 2013).

Anxiety- and Depressive-Like Behavior

In the last two decades, many rodent studies have considered associations between PS and offspring anxiety- and depressive-like behavior in the offspring. The hyperactivity of the HPA axis induced by PS is very often related to behavioral changes in the offspring (Zagron & Weinstock, 2006). The findings range from increased ultrasonic vocalizations (USV) in infancy (Laloux et al., 2012). PS rats produce significantly more USV in response to postnatal isolation compared to controls. Furthermore, PS reduced exploration behavior of the offspring in the elevated-plus maze test and open field test (Vallee et al., 1997) and increased immobility in the Porsolt test during (Morley-Fletcher, Darnaudery, et al., 2003). Many of these findings show distinct sex differences (Bowman et al., 2004; Brunton & Russell, 2010; Schroeder, Sultany, & Weller, 2013). Nevertheless it is not clear, which gender is more susceptible to PS. Taken together, evidence supports the hypothesis that PS exposure proliferates anxiety- and depression-like behavior in rat offspring. Rodent models of PS can therefore be used to replicate developmental factors involved in the etiology of anxiety or depressive disorders (Mairesse et al., 2015). Moreover, these animal models allow proving treatment strategies. For example, resulted enrichment of the postnatal environment (early handling) (Morley-Fletcher, Rea, Maccari, & Laviola, 2003). Concordant with these results did a treatment with antidepressants totally reverse the behavioral changes induced by PS (Buhl et al., 2010; Morley-Fletcher, Darnaudery, et al., 2003).

Social Behavior

The PS models on fear, anxiety, or depression-like behavior show also interconnections with aggressive or antisocial behavior. Male PS offspring showed reduced social play during adolescence. Lee, Brady, Shapiro, Dorsa, and Koenig (2007) report that PS exposure diminished the quality of the social interaction behavior in offspring. Moreover, they found less oxytocin mRNA in the paraventricular nucleus and increased oxytocin receptor binding in the central amygdala. Oxytocin administration into the central amygdala reversed the social incompetence of the PS rats.

Learning and Memory

Structural changes in the hippocampus and amygdala can also be linked to learning or memory impairments. The study by Bowman et al. (2004) discovered that PS offspring had no deficits in object recognition, but instead males lost their advantage in spatial memory. Markham, Taylor, Taylor, Bell, and Koenig (2010) found that PS males were impaired on every task a cognitive battery (Novel object recognition task, Contextual fear conditioning, Morris Water Maze, "Can Test"). Other studies using the Morris water maze have shown that PS impairs spatial memory significantly (Barzegar, Sajjadi, Talaei, Hamidi, & Salami, 2015). In agreement with previous work Benoit, Rakic, and Frick (2015) also found that generally impaired spatial memory in the Morris water maze.

Cognitive deficits induced by PS are linked to a reduced hippocampal neurogenesis, and were reversible by treatments with antidepressants (Morley-Fletcher et al., 2011) or the neurotrophin, insulin-like growth factor 1 (Darnaudery, Perez-Martin, Belizaire, Maccari, & Garcia-Segura, 2006).

Postnatal Stress

Not only fetal environment but also early childhood influences the stress systems. Levine, Alpert, and Lewis (1957) and afterwards many other research groups have demonstrated that GC responses to stress were modulated by ELS in rats and result in stable changes of the HPA-axis reactivity. Rodent models on the ELS are also commonly used to study the development of psychiatric disorders such as anxiety and depression (Davidson & McEwen, 2012).

Due to the fact that rat pups are dependent on maternal care for survival, prenatal stress paradigms use short (3 min) to long-lasting (no contact to the mother) separations to stimulate stress. As presented in Table 2, there are three main postnatal stress models: early handling (EH), maternal separation (MS), and maternal deprivation (MD). Brief separations (3–15 min) are a very mild stressor for the pub and may result in increased maternal care, which could have in sum a positive effect on the development of the offspring (Claessens, Daskalakis, Oitzl, & de Kloet, 2012; Liu et al., 1997).

In contrast, prolonged separations or MD causes a significant amount of stress and a hyperreactivity of the HPA axis in the offspring. Nevertheless, medium to longer separations, which are particularly stressful for the dams, may produce greater interest by the mother in the pups after reunion. The results of ELS studies with rodents depend not only on the type, intensity, and frequency of the stressors, but also on the species (mice vs. rats) and on the timing of the ELS (at the beginning or at the end of the hyporesponsive postpartum period) (Roque, Mesquita, Palha, Sousa, & Correia-Neves, 2014). During this period (postnatal days 4–14; Enthoven et al., 2010) rats or mice exhibit a reduced response to stress, manifested by a reduced secretion of ACTH and CORT in response to stress (Levine, 2002).

HPA-Axis Functioning

Several studies have shown that the quality of maternal care or the intensity of licking and grooming behavior (LG) early in life is associated with the HPA-axis responsivity in adult rats. Compared to the adult offspring of Low LG mothers, the offspring of High LG mothers have lower plasma Cortisol and ACTH levels (Liu et al., 1997). The authors found an upregulation of hippocampal glucocorticoid receptors (GR) in the offspring of High LG mothers. Since the hippocampus plays a central role in the

Table 2. Models to induce postnatal stress in rodents

Early Handling Model (EH) The EH Model allows researchers to study the influence of different early environmental factors (maternal care, maternal separation, novelty exposure, tactile stimulation) on the outcome phenotype of the rat offspring. It combines a daily handling of the rat pup by the researcher with a maternal separation during the neonatal phase. In this model, litters are removed from their home cage/their mother and receive a handling for 3–60 min. In general, early handling is carried out directly after birth and continued through the first postnatal weeks.
Maternal Separation Model (MS) The MS Model may be performed in different ways that induce varying degrees of stress. The effect of the separation is a function of the frequency and duration as well as the rat pup's age and gender. Another important influencing factor on the outcome of MS is, besides the light cycle and the ambient temperature, the reaction of the mother during reunion phase. In most studies, the mother is removed from the home cage, leaving the litter without care but in its familiar environment once or twice daily. Separations, usually lasting 180–360 min, but also separations of 24 hrs have been used. Alternatively, a single separation for a longer period of time can be used.
Maternal Deprivation Model (MD) The MD Model is the most powerful model to induce postnatal stress in rodents. In this model, the rat pup is transferred into a new environment in which it is deprived not only of the mother but also of its familiar environment. The deprivation can last between 1 hrs daily from the second day postpartum up to a complete separation, rearing the litter without any further contact to the dam with intragastric feeding.

association between ELS and modifications of the HPA-axis activity, these changes may have wide-ranging consequences for emotions, behavior, learning, and adaptation.

Brief MSs increase the frequency of maternal interaction and caring behaviors, which promotes the GR expression in the hippocampus and the prefrontal cortex (Melo, 2015). The increased availability of GRs attenuates the responsivity of the HPA axis resulting in a reduced GC release in response to stress (George, Stout, Tan, Knox, & Liberzon, 2013), less anxiety-like behaviors (Skripuletz, Kruschinski, Pabst, von Horsten, & Stephan, 2010), and better memory functions (Plescia et al., 2014). Handled offspring showed also a decreased emotional arousal (Darnaudery, Dutriez, Viltart, Morley-Fletcher, & Maccari, 2004), which may be related to a diminution in the branching of dendrites in the locus coeruleus (Lucion, Pereira, Winkelman, Sanvitto, & Anselmo-Franci, 2003; Plotsky et al., 2005). Data also demonstrate that very brief separations followed by increased maternal care decrease the mortality of stressed rats that were separated from their mothers as neonates (Coutellier, Friedrich, Failing, & Wurbel, 2008; Pickering, Gustafsson, Cebere, Nylander, & Liljequist, 2006).

While EH or short separations of the pubs act more as protective factors by reducing the impact of ELS, longer separations have adverse effects on the HPA-axis reactivity and hence also on behavioral outcomes (Bailoo, Jordan, Garza, & Tyler, 2014). Data indicate that MS in rodents causes important HPA-axis dysregulations in adulthood, as reflected in increased CRH gene expression in several brain areas (Wang et al., 2014), and in an increased responsiveness of ACTH and CORT to acute stressors (Liu, Caldji, Sharma, Plotsky, & Meaney, 2000). Maternally separated (longer than 15 min) offspring, as compared to handled pubs (separated for 3–15 min) or controls, display an increased stress responsiveness, changes in the GR gene and CRH gene expression, especially in the hippocampus, the prefrontal cortex, and the locus coeruleus (Liebl et al., 2009; Pan, Fleming, Lawson, Jenkins, & McGowan, 2014). These changes were related to behavioral changes like enhanced emotional reactivity and anxiety, but also to impaired cognitive performance in later life (Maniam & Morris, 2010).

Anxiety- and Depressive-Like Behavior

It seems reasonable to assume that the programming effects of ELS on amygdala functions and in stress-sensitive brain regions cause anxiety-like or depression-like behavior in rats (Davidson & McEwen, 2012). Low LG induces in offspring a depression-like phenotype, which was also seen in rats after chronic stress. Depression-like behaviors in Low LG offspring were associated with a reduced GC negative-feedback sensitivity and increased HPA-axis responses to stress as well as increased fearfulness and increased immobility different paradigms for the testing of anxiety-like or depression-like behavior (Elevated Plus Maze, Porsolt test, Open Field test; compare Table 3) (Connors, Migliore, Pillsbury, Shaik, & Kentner, 2015; Fuentes et al., 2014).

Social Behavior

Compared to the many studies assessing the impact of ELS on anxiety-like or depressive-like behavior, aggressive behavior is neglected in research. Cordero et al. (2012) could show that male rats became highly aggressive against their female partners as adults when they were exposed to fear-inducing stress during their peripuberty. Their offspring also showed increased aggression toward females in the absence of postnatal father-offspring interaction or any other exposure to violence. Both the females that cohabited with the stressed males (F0) as well those that cohabited with their male offspring (F1) showed behavioral (including anxiety- and depression-like behaviors), physiological (decreased body weight and basal corticosterone levels), and neurobiological symptoms (increased activity in dorsal raphe serotonergic neurons in response to an unfamiliar male). Another study used MS (3 hrs daily on postnatal day 1–14) and found altered adult emotionality including impaired social behavior, enhanced aggression, and violence in adult (Veenema, Blume, Niederle, Buwalda, & Neumann, 2006) as well in juvenile rats (Veenema & Neumann, 2009). The juvenile rats showed also an increase in attacks, offensive pulling and biting, and a lower frequency of submissive play behaviors. Furthermore, MS rats showed higher plasma corticosterone levels and higher vasopressin mRNA expression in the paraventricular nucleus.

Memory and Learning

As a result of the changes in the HPA axis and the impaired synaptic plasticity caused by early maternal behavior or MS, we see also effects on hippocampus-dependent learning. In line with the findings on high or low maternal care, studies with rats found similar effects on memory and learning for MS. The separation from the mother impaired spatial learning, memory ability, and LTP in the hippocampus of adolescent rats, but there was timing effect. Early as well late MS was associated with lower LTP values compared to the control group, but only the separation between postnatal day 14–21 (late) resulted in a significant worst performance in the Morris Water Maze compared to controls or early (postnatal day 2–9) separated pubs (Cao et al., 2014). While offspring of High LG mothers acquires the location of a hidden platform in the Morris water maze more rapidly (Bredy, Zhang, Grant, Diorio, & Meaney, 2004) and shows enhanced memory in an object recognition task (Plescia et al., 2014). Consistent with the positive effects on hippocampal-dependent learning and memory, long-term potentiation (LTP) in the hippocampus (DG, CA1) is increased in High LG offspring compared to Low LG offspring (Bagot et al., 2012). Lukas, Bredewold,

Table 3. Methods to assess stress outcomes in offspring

The Social Interaction Test During the Social Interaction Test the rat is allowed to explore the home cage of an unfamiliar congener or to interact with the congener in a neutral environment. Social exploration is measured by the time spent around the congener as well as the amount and duration of behaviors that comprise social interaction (e.g., following, sniffing, grooming, climbing, biting, fighting). This paradigm is used to assess anxiety, aggression, depressive-like behavior, or social behavior.
The Forced Swim Test (Porsolt Test, PST) The PST was developed to assess depressive-like behaviors (learned helplessness) in rodents. In this paradigm, the animal is placed in a cylindrical container of water, deep enough so that the animal cannot touch the bottom with its tail or feet, and from which it cannot escape. Normally the rodent will attempt to escape by actively swimming. When the animal stops swimming and floats on the surface of the water it is assumed to have "given up." "Giving up" very quickly is thought to be a depressive-like behavior.
Elevated Plus Maze The Elevated Plus Maze consists of a "+"-shaped maze with two oppositely positioned closed and two oppositely positioned open arms. The rodent is allowed to freely explore the maze. This paradigm is used to assess anxiety. Anxious behavior is defined as a preference for being in closed arms. This preference is calculated by the percentage of entries or time spent in the open arms in relation to time or entries in closed arms.
Y-Maze The Y-Maze is a Y-shaped apparatus that includes an elevated open alley. Like the Elevated Plus Maze, this paradigm is used to assess anxiety in rodents as the ratio between open arm entries and closed arm entries.
Open Field Test The Open Field test is a simple sensorimotor test in which the rodent is placed in the center of a square, white Plexiglas box. The animal is allowed to freely explore the box for about 10 min while being recorded by a video tracking system. The movement is analyzed for the distance moved, velocity, and time spent in predefined zones. The Open Field test is used to assess general activity levels, locomotor activity, and anxious behavior (defined as little exploration).
The Morris Water Maze The Morris Water Maze is a large round tub filled with opaque water (by adding tempera or powdered milk) with two small hidden platforms located 1–2 cm under the water surface. The rodent is placed repeatedly on a start platform and normally it swims around until it finds another platform to rest on. While swimming, the rodent is monitored by a video tracking system. This paradigm is designed to assess memory by measuring the time it takes for a rat to find the hidden platform. Observed parameters are: latency, distance moved, and velocity.

Landgraf, Neumann, and Veenema (2011) found that MS impairs social recognition performance in the social discrimination test in juvenile (5-week-old) and adult (16-week-old) male rats. Furthermore, the impaired social recognition may also explain deficits in social behaviors like aggression as shown previously (Veenema & Neumann, 2009).

The Epigenetic Basis of Early-Life Programming

It is widely accepted that mental health problems are determined by complex interactions between genes and an individual's experiences or its environment. Several studies show a biological interplay between environmental signals and the genome in the regulation of individual differences in behavior, cognition, and physiology.

Data suggest that dynamic epigenetic changes, molecular modifications that alter gene expressions without altering the underlying DNA sequence, explain this plasticity. Such sustained effects of the environment on the genome appear everywhere in biology, including plants, mammals, insects, or fish, and may have developed to prepare the offspring on an environment that the offspring will likely face as adults.

There are four main epigenetic mechanisms: DNA methylation, histone modification, chromatin remodeling, and noncoding RNA-mediated modifications. DNA methylation is the most widely investigated and best-understood epigenetic change. These alterations are realized by DNA methylations and hydroxymethylations, enzymatic (by DNA methyltransferase; DNMT) catalyzed binding processes of methyl groups to the cytosine bases of the DNA, to lock genes "off." Histone proteins are modulated by a large set of chemical reactions such as methylation, acetylation, or phosphorylation.

Chromatin structure is modulated through altering the positioning of nucleosomes. In addition, epigenetic regulation of gene function also involves noncoding and microRNAs, which act on mRNA stability and translation process. The exact role of these epigenetic changes in gene expression is still not fully understood, but it is clear that DNA methylation is essential for cell differentiation and embryonic development. Methylation seems to play a mediating role in gene expression, with more methylation of promoters, a specific region of the DNA that initiates the gene

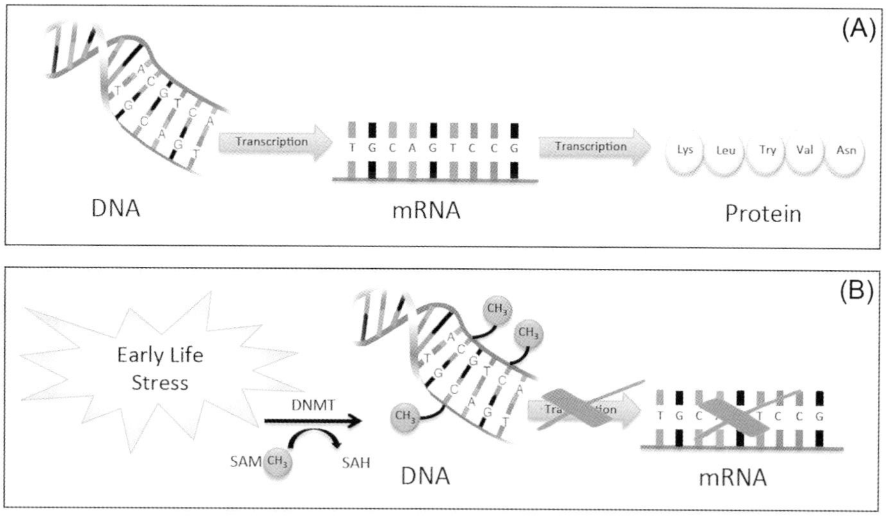

Figure 1. Gene regulation by DNA methylation. (A) The activity of genes is determined by the level transcribed DNA to messenger RNA (mRNA). Within the ribosome, the mRNA (which carries the coding sequences for the protein synthesis) directs the protein synthesis (merging together of amino acids). (B) Earl Life stress initiates DNA methylation mechanisms. The DNA methyltransferase (DNMT) catalyzes the transfer of a methyl group from S-adenosylmethionine (SAM) to the cytosine bases in DNA, which are methylated into 5-methylcytosine. The methylation of cytosine at critical positions in the DNS silences the transcription of DNA, thus converting an active gene to an inactive gene.

transcription, correlating with low or no transcription of the genome (Suzuki & Bird, 2008) (Figure 1).

Data suggest that the early-life environment changes epigenetic structures of an individual and may be transferred through generations (Desplats, 2015; Franklin et al., 2010). The epigenetic programming of early-life experience in the rodent was first time demonstrated by the group of Michael Meaney (Fish et al., 2004; Weaver et al., 2001). The researchers used the already described variations of rat mothers' maternal care behavior. They found that differences in maternal care resulted in differences in histone acetylation DNA methylation of the GR exon promoter. These studies showed the first time that maternal behavior results in DNA methylation changes in a GR promoter region and affects GR expression. This epigenetic alteration of the GR in turn affects the HPA-axis activity. Similarly, ELS in mice causes sustained DNA hypomethylation of the arginine vasopressin (AVP) gene underpinning sustained expression and increased HPA-axis activity (Murgatroyd & Spengler, 2011). Subsequently, many more studies on epigenetic programming have used rodent models to study the epigenetic fundament of Early-Life Programming (Babenko et al., 2015; Desplats, 2015; Turecki & Meaney, 2014; Tyrka et al., 2015).

Although, epigenetic changes are rather long term and stable, demethylation as an "epigenetic reprogramming" is possible. Further research proposed, that the hypermethylation of several sites caused by ELS is reversible in adult life. For instance, Weaver et al. (2005) could reverse the DNA methylation effect of maternal care by injections of amino acid L-methionine that serves as the donor of methyl groups for DNA methylation. The differences in adult behavior (e.g., anxiety) as a result of maternal care in early life were reversible in both directions by agents that stimulate DNA methylation (L-methionine) or DNA demethylation (Trichostatin A) (Weaver, Meaney, & Szyf, 2006). Other studies used maternal tactile stimulation (LG behavior) to reverse epigenetic modifications of the HPA stress responsivity. Liberman et al. (2012) demonstrated that postnatal maternal care could change the of DNA methylation profiles in mouse models. In this study a demethylation of the GR promoter was correlated with increased maternal care in juvenile mice.

Recent evidence suggests that three enzyme families play a critical role in DNA demethylation: (a) the 10–11 translocation (TET) family, (b) the activation-induced cytidine deaminase (AID)/APOBEC family, and (c) the base excision repair (BER) family have been identified as having roles in active DNA demethylation (Bhutani, Burns, & Blau, 2011).

One of the most investigated candidates is the AID (Shoemaker, Wang, & Zhang, 2011; Teperek-Tkacz, Pasque, Gentsch, & Ferguson-Smith, 2011). After deamination, the DNA has a mismatch and is repaired. The AID repairs guanine/thymine mismatches efficiently. This activity leads to DNA demethylation. But in fact, studies have also shown that AID was involved not only in DNA methylation, but also in demethylation (Maccari et al., 2014).

Conclusions

Taken together, this review has illustrated, on the basis of rodent studies, the profound and long-lasting effects of ELS. The developing brain is plastic in response to environmental influences. Pre- and postnatal stress produces modifications in brain regions such as the hippocampus, amygdala, and prefrontal cortex, which are associated with mood- and anxiety-related behaviors, as well as cognitive functions in rodent models. On the other hand, this review highlights the possible strategies to revers the negative impact of ELS like good maternal care enriched environments, antidepressants, or oxytocin administrations.

Because of the negative outcome phenotypes of pre- and postnatal stress, an understanding of the central mechanisms in human beings is important to pave the way for new treatments and prevention. DNA methylation serves as one mechanism that explains the association between early stressful experiences and outcome phenotypes. A reasonable link that explains DNA methylation across tissues are the circulating stress hormones such as GCs, which are released in response to ELS. Laboratory studies with rodents have shown that DNA methylation and histone modification explain the association between prenatal stress, MS, maternal care, and behavioral outcomes.

The translation from rodent models to the human condition is becoming possible, for instance, with brain imaging or epigenetic techniques. For human beings, there is epidemiologic evidence for fetal programming of many illnesses, including psychopathologies (Beijers, Jansen, Riksen-Walraven, & de Weerth, 2010; Colman, Ataullahjan, Naicker, & Van Lieshout, 2012; Loomans et al., 2011; Zohsel et al., 2014), but the precise mechanisms underlying prenatal stress are not fully understood. More extensively studied in human beings is the impact of postnatal stress. Childhood adversity has been linked to later psychopathology (Alkon et al., 2014; Carr, Martins, Stingel, Lemgruber, & Juruena, 2013); other studies have illuminated the neuroendocrine and neurobiological mechanisms (McGowan, 2012; Szyf, 2013; Tyrka et al., 2015).

Given the fact that ELS has such profound consequences on health and disease, prevention and intervention programs should target this critical phase of development. As shown in animal studies, DNA methylation and histone acetylation are reversible biochemical reactions and should therefore be targeted by psychotherapeutic or pharmacological interventions. The treatment of problems that arise as the consequence of adverse experiences early in life or to promote better outcomes after such adverse experiences requires tremendous efforts and cost, and will possibly not be as effective. On the other side, prevention programs to reduce ELS, especially childhood abuse, neglect, or trauma, are complex and require commitment and expenditures by governments, but in the long run they are the most cost-effective way of making a difference.

Acknowledgment

The author indicates that she has no financial relationships and conflict of interests relevant to this article disclose.

References

Alkon, A., Boyce, W. T., Tran, L., Harley, K. G., Neuhaus, J., & Eskenazi, B. (2014). Prenatal adversities and Latino children's autonomic nervous system reactivity trajectories from 6 months to 5 years of age. *PLoS One, 9*, e86283. doi: 10.1371/journal.pone.0086283

Babenko, O., Kovalchuk, I., & Metz, G. A. (2015). Stress-induced perinatal and transgenerational epigenetic programming of brain development and mental health. *Neuroscience and Biobehavioral Reviews, 48*, 70–91. doi: 10.1016/j.neubiorev.2014.11.013

Bagot, R. C., Tse, Y. C., Nguyen, H. B., Wong, A. S., Meaney, M. J., & Wong, T. P. (2012). Maternal care influences hippocampal N-methyl-D-aspartate receptor function and dynamic regulation by corticosterone in adulthood. *Biological Psychiatry, 72*, 491–498. doi: 10.1016/j.biopsych.2012.03.016

Bailoo, J. D., Jordan, R. L., Garza, X. J., & Tyler, A. N. (2014). Brief and long periods of maternal separation affect maternal behavior and offspring behavioral development in C57BL/6 mice. *Developmental Psychobiology, 56*, 674–685. doi: 10.1002/dev.21135

Barker, D. J. (1993). Fetal origins of coronary heart disease. *British Heart Journal, 69*, 195–196.

Barnes, S. K., & Ozanne, S. E. (2011). Pathways linking the early environment to long-term health and lifespan. *Progress in Biophysics and Molecular Biology, 106*, 323–336. doi: 10.1016/j.pbiomolbio.2010.12.005

Barzegar, M., Sajjadi, F. S., Talaei, S. A., Hamidi, G., & Salami, M. (2015). Prenatal exposure to noise stress: Anxiety, impaired spatial memory, and deteriorated hippocampal plasticity in postnatal life. *Hippocampus, 25*, 187–196. doi: 10.1002/hipo.22363

Beijers, R., Jansen, J., Riksen-Walraven, M., & de Weerth, C. (2010). Maternal prenatal anxiety and stress predict infant illnesses and health complaints. *Pediatrics, 126*, e401–e409. doi: 10.1542/peds.2009-3226

Belay, H., Burton, C. L., Lovic, V., Meaney, M. J., Sokolowski, M., & Fleming, A. S. (2011). Early adversity and serotonin transporter genotype interact with hippocampal glucocorticoid receptor mRNA expression, corticosterone, and behavior in adult male rats. *Behavioral Neuroscience, 125*, 150–160. doi: 10.1037/a0022891

Benoit, J. D., Rakic, P., & Frick, K. M. (2015). Prenatal stress induces spatial memory deficits and epigenetic changes in the hippocampus indicative of heterochromatin formation and reduced gene expression. *Behavioral Brain Research, 281*, 1–8. doi: 10.1016/j.bbr.2014.12.001

Bhatnagar, S., Lee, T. M., & Vining, C. (2005). Prenatal stress differentially affects habituation of corticosterone responses to repeated stress in adult male and female rats. *Hormones and Behavior, 47*, 430–438. doi: 10.1016/j.yhbeh.2004.11.019

Bhutani, N., Burns, D. M., & Blau, H. M. (2011). DNA demethylation dynamics. *Cell, 146*, 866–872. doi: 10.1016/j.cell.2011.08.042

Bowman, R. E., MacLusky, N. J., Sarmiento, Y., Frankfurt, M., Gordon, M., & Luine, V. N. (2004). Sexually dimorphic effects of prenatal stress on cognition, hormonal responses, and central neurotransmitters. *Endocrinology, 145*, 3778–3787. doi: 10.1210/en.2003-1759

Branchi, I., & Cirulli, F. (2014). Early experiences: Building up the tools to face the challenges of adult life. *Developmental Psychobiology, 56*, 1661–1674. doi: 10.1002/dev.21235

Bredy, T. W., Zhang, T. Y., Grant, R. J., Diorio, J., & Meaney, M. J. (2004). Peripubertal environmental enrichment reverses the effects of maternal care on hippocampal development and glutamate receptor subunit expression. *European Journal of Neuroscience, 20*, 1355–1362. doi: 10.1111/j.1460-9568.2004.03599.x

Brunton, P. J., & Russell, J. A. (2010). Prenatal social stress in the rat programmes neuroendocrine and behavioural responses to stress in the adult offspring: Sex-specific effects. *Journal of Neuroendocrinology, 22*, 258–271. doi: 10.1111/j.1365-2826.2010.01969.x

Buhl, E. S., Jensen, T. K., Jessen, N., Elfving, B., Buhl, C. S., Kristiansen, S. B., . . . Petersen, K. F. (2010). Treatment with an SSRI antidepressant restores hippocampo-hypothalamic corticosteroid feedback and reverses insulin resistance in low-birth-weight rats. *American Journal of Physiology – Endocrinology and Metabolism, 298*, E920–E929. doi: 10.1152/ajpendo.00606.2009

Cao, X., Huang, S., Cao, J., Chen, T., Zhu, P., Zhu, R., . . . Ruan, D. (2014). The timing of maternal separation affects morris water maze performance and long-term potentiation in male rats. *Developmental Psychobiology, 56*, 1102–1109. doi: 10.1002/dev.21130

Carr, C. P., Martins, C. M., Stingel, A. M., Lemgruber, V. B., & Juruena, M. F. (2013). The role of early life stress in adult psychiatric disorders: A systematic review according to childhood trauma subtypes. *Journal of Nervous and Mental Disease, 201*, 1007–1020. doi: 10.1097/NMD.0000000000000049

Champagne, F. A. (2013). Early environments, glucocorticoid receptors, and behavioral epigenetics. *Behavioral Neuroscience, 127*, 628–636. doi: 10.1037/a0034186

Champagne, F. A., Francis, D. D., Mar, A., & Meaney, M. J. (2003). Variations in maternal care in the rat as a mediating influence for the effects of environment on development. *Physiology and Behavior, 79*, 359–371.

Claessens, S. E., Daskalakis, N. P., Oitzl, M. S., & de Kloet, E. R. (2012). Early handling modulates outcome of neonatal dexamethasone exposure. *Hormones and Behavior, 62*, 433–441. doi: 10.1016/j.yhbeh.2012.07.011

Colman, I., Ataullahjan, A., Naicker, K., & Van Lieshout, R. J. (2012). Birth weight, stress, and symptoms of depression in adolescence: Evidence of fetal programming in a national Canadian cohort. *Canadian Journal of Psychiatry, 57*, 422–428.

Connors, E. J., Migliore, M. M., Pillsbury, S. L., Shaik, A. N., & Kentner, A. C. (2015). Environmental enrichment models a naturalistic form of maternal separation and shapes the anxiety response patterns of offspring. *Psychoneuroendocrinology, 52*, 153–167. doi: 10.1016/j.psyneuen.2014.10.021

Cordero, M. I., Poirier, G. L., Marquez, C., Veenit, V., Fontana, X., Salehi, B., . . . Sandi, C. (2012). Evidence for biological roots in the transgenerational transmission of intimate partner violence. *Translational Psychiatry, 2*, e106. doi: 10.1038/tp.2012.32

Coutellier, L., Friedrich, A. C., Failing, K., & Wurbel, H. (2008). Variations in the postnatal maternal environment in mice: Effects on maternal behaviour and behavioural and endocrine responses in the adult offspring. *Physiology and Behavior, 93*, 395–407. doi: 10.1016/j.physbeh.2007.09.008

Darnaudery, M., Dutriez, I., Viltart, O., Morley-Fletcher, S., & Maccari, S. (2004). Stress during gestation induces lasting effects on emotional reactivity of the dam rat. *Behavioral Brain Research, 153*, 211–216. doi: 10.1016/j.bbr.2003.12.001

Darnaudery, M., Perez-Martin, M., Belizaire, G., Maccari, S., & Garcia-Segura, L. M. (2006). Insulin-likc growth factor 1 reduces age-related disorders induced by prenatal stress in female rats. *Neurobiology of Aging, 27*, 119–127. doi: 10.1016/j.neurobiolaging.2005.01.008

Davidson, R. J., & McEwen, B. S. (2012). Social influences on neuroplasticity: Stress and interventions to promote well-being. *Nature Neuroscience, 15*, 689–695. doi: 10.1038/nn.3093

Desplats, P. A. (2015). Perinatal programming of neurodevelopment: Epigenetic mechanisms and the prenatal shaping of the brain. *Advances in Neurobiology, 10*, 335–361. doi: 10.1007/978-1-4939-1372-5_16

Enthoven, L., Schmidt, M. V., Cheung, Y. H., van der Mark, M. H., de Kloet, E. R., & Oitzl, M. S. (2010). Ontogeny of the HPA axis of the CD1 mouse following 24 h maternal deprivation at pnd 3. *International Journal of Developmental Neuroscience, 28*, 217–224. doi: 10.1016/j.ijdevneu.2009.10.006

Fish, E. W., Shahrokh, D., Bagot, R., Caldji, C., Bredy, T., Szyf, M., & Meaney, M. J. (2004). Epigenetic programming of stress responses through variations in maternal care. *Annals of the New York Academy of Sciences, 1036*, 167–180. doi: 10.1196/annals.1330.011

Franklin, T. B., Russig, H., Weiss, I. C., Graff, J., Linder, N., Michalon, A., . . . Mansuy, I. M. (2010). Epigenetic transmission of the impact of early stress across generations. *Biological Psychiatry, 68*, 408–415. doi: 10.1016/j.biopsych.2010.05.036

Fuentes, S., Daviu, N., Gagliano, H., Garrido, P., Zelena, D., Monasterio, N., . . . Nadal, R. (2014). Sex-dependent effects of an early life treatment in rats that increases maternal care: Vulnerability or resilience? *Frontiers in Behavioral Neuroscience, 8*, 56. doi: 10.3389/fnbeh.2014.00056

Garcia-Caceres, C., Lagunas, N., Calmarza-Font, I., Azcoitia, I., Diz-Chaves, Y., Garcia-Segura, L. M., . . . Chowen, J. A. (2010). Gender differences in the long-term effects of chronic prenatal stress on the HPA axis and hypothalamic structure in rats. *Psychoneuroendocrinology, 35*, 1525–1535. doi: 10.1016/j.psyneuen.2010.05.006

George, S. A., Stout, S. A., Tan, M., Knox, D., & Liberzon, I. (2013). Early handling attenuates enhancement of glucocorticoid receptors in the prefrontal cortex in an animal model of post-traumatic stress disorder. *Biology of Mood & Anxiety Disorders, 3*, 22. doi: 10.1186/2045-5380-3-22

Green, M. K., Rani, C. S., Joshi, A., Soto-Pina, A. E., Martinez, P. A., Frazer, A., . . . Morilak, D. A. (2011). Prenatal stress induces long term stress vulnerability, compromising stress response systems in the brain and impairing extinction of conditioned fear after adult stress. *Neuroscience, 192*, 438–451. doi: 10.1016/j.neuroscience.2011.06.041

Kapoor, A., Petropoulos, S., & Matthews, S. G. (2008). Fetal programming of hypothalamic-pituitary-adrenal (HPA) axis function and behavior by synthetic glucocorticoids. *Brain Research Reviews, 57*, 586–595. doi: 10.1016/j.brainresrev.2007.06.013

Koehl, M., Darnaudery, M., Dulluc, J., Van Reeth, O., Le Moal, M., & Maccari, S. (1999). Prenatal stress alters circadian activity of hypothalamo-pituitary-adrenal axis and hippocampal corticosteroid receptors in adult rats of both gender. *Journal of Neurobiology, 40*, 302–315.

Laloux, C., Mairesse, J., Van Camp, G., Giovine, A., Branchi, I., Bouret, S., . . . Maccari, S. (2012). Anxiety-like behaviour and associated neurochemical and endocrinological alterations in male pups exposed to prenatal stress. *Psychoneuroendocrinology, 37*, 1646–1658. doi: 10.1016/j.psyneuen.2012.02.010

Lee, P. R., Brady, D. L., Shapiro, R. A., Dorsa, D. M., & Koenig, J. I. (2007). Prenatal stress generates deficits in rat social behavior: Reversal by oxytocin. *Brain Research, 1156*, 152–167. doi: 10.1016/j.brainres.2007.04.042

Levine, S. (2002). Regulation of the hypothalamic-pituitary-adrenal axis in the neonatal rat: The role of maternal behavior. *Neurotoxicity Research, 4*, 557–564. doi: 10.1080/10298420290030569

Levine, S., Alpert, M., & Lewis, G. W. (1957). Infantile experience and the maturation of the pituitary adrenal axis. *Science, 126*, 1347.

Liberman, S. A., Mashoodh, R., Thompson, R. C., Dolinoy, D. C., & Champagne, F. A. (2012). Concordance in hippocampal and fecal Nr3c1 methylation is moderated by maternal behavior in the mouse. *Ecology and Evolution, 2*, 3123–3131. doi: 10.1002/ece3.416

Liebl, C., Panhuysen, M., Putz, B., Trumbach, D., Wurst, W., Deussing, J. M., . . . Schmidt, M. V. (2009). Gene expression profiling following maternal deprivation: Involvement of the brain Renin-Angiotensin system. *Frontiers in Molecular Neuroscience, 2*, 1. doi: 10.3389/neuro.02.001.2009

Liu, D., Caldji, C., Sharma, S., Plotsky, P. M., & Meaney, M. J. (2000). Influence of neonatal rearing conditions on stress-induced adrenocorticotropin responses and norepinepherine release in the hypothalamic paraventricular nucleus. *Journal of Neuroendocrinology, 12*, 5–12.

Liu, D., Diorio, J., Tannenbaum, B., Caldji, C., Francis, D., Freedman, A., . . . Meaney, M. J. (1997). Maternal care, hippocampal glucocorticoid receptors, and hypothalamic-pituitary-adrenal responses to stress. *Science, 277*, 1659–1662.

Loomans, E. M., van der Stelt, O., van Eijsden, M., Gemke, R. J., Vrijkotte, T., & den Bergh, B. R. (2011). Antenatal maternal anxiety is associated with problem behaviour at age five. *Early Human Development, 87*, 565–570. doi: 10.1016/j.earlhumdev.2011.04.014

Lu, X., Jin, C., Yang, J., Liu, Q., Wu, S., Li, D., . . . Cai, Y. (2013). Prenatal and lactational lead exposure enhanced oxidative stress and altered apoptosis status in offspring rats' hippocampus. *Biological Trace Element Research, 151*, 75–84. doi: 10.1007/s12011-012-9531-5

Lucion, A. B., Pereira, F. M., Winkelman, E. C., Sanvitto, G. L., & Anselmo-Franci, J. A. (2003). Neonatal handling reduces the number of cells in the locus coeruleus of rats. *Behavioral Neuroscience, 117*, 894–903. doi: 10.1037/0735-7044.117.5.894

Lukas, M., Bredewold, R., Landgraf, R., Neumann, I. D., & Veenema, A. H. (2011). Early life stress impairs social recognition due to a blunted response of vasopressin release within the septum of adult male rats. *Psychoneuroendocrinology, 36*, 843–853. doi: 10.1016/j.psyneuen.2010.11.007

Maccari, S., Darnaudery, M., Morley-Fletcher, S., Zuena, A. R., Cinque, C., & Van Reeth, O. (2003). Prenatal stress and long-term consequences: implications of glucocorticoid hormones. *Neuroscience & Biobehavioral Reviews, 27*, 119–127.

Maccari, S., Krugers, H. J., Morley-Fletcher, S., Szyf, M., & Brunton, P. J. (2014). The consequences of early-life adversity: Neurobiological, behavioural and epigenetic adaptations. *Journal of Neuroendocrinology, 26*, 707–723. doi: 10.1111/jne.12175

Mairesse, J., Van Camp, G., Gatta, E., Marrocco, J., Reynaert, M. L., Consolazione, M., . . . Maccari, S. (2015). Sleep in prenatally restraint stressed rats, a model of mixed anxiety-depressive disorder. *Advances in Neurobiology, 10*, 27–44. doi: 10.1007/978-1-4939-1372-5_2

Maniam, J., & Morris, M. J. (2010). Palatable cafeteria diet ameliorates anxiety and depression-like symptoms following an adverse early environment. *Psychoneuroendocrinology, 35*, 717–728. doi: 10.1016/j.psyneuen.2009.10.013

Markham, J. A., Taylor, A. R., Taylor, S. B., Bell, D. B., & Koenig, J. I. (2010). Characterization of the cognitive impairments induced by prenatal exposure to stress in the rat. *Frontiers in Behavioral Neuroscience, 4*, 173. doi: 10.3389/fnbeh.2010.00173

McGowan, P. O. (2012). Epigenetic clues to the biological embedding of early life adversity. *Biological Psychiatry, 72*, 4–5. doi: 10.1016/j.biopsych.2012.04.017

Melo, A. I. (2015). Role of sensory, social, and hormonal signals from the mother on the development of offspring. *Advances in Neurobiology, 10*, 219–248. doi: 10.1007/978-1-4939-1372-5_11

Morley-Fletcher, S., Darnaudery, M., Koehl, M., Casolini, P., Van Reeth, O., & Maccari, S. (2003). Prenatal stress in rats predicts immobility behavior in the forced swim test. *Effects of a chronic treatment with tianeptine. Brain Research, 989*, 246–251.

Morley-Fletcher, S., Mairesse, J., Soumier, A., Banasr, M., Fagioli, F., Gabriel, C., . . . Maccari, S. (2011). Chronic agomelatine treatment corrects behavioral, cellular, and biochemical abnormalities induced by prenatal stress in rats. *Psychopharmacology (Berl), 217*, 301–313. doi: 10.1007/s00213-011-2280-x

Morley-Fletcher, S., Rea, M., Maccari, S., & Laviola, G. (2003). Environmental enrichment during adolescence reverses the effects of prenatal stress on play behaviour and HPA axis reactivity in rats. *The European Journal of Neuroscience, 18*, 3367–3374.

Murgatroyd, C., & Spengler, D. (2011). Epigenetic programming of the HPA axis: Early life decides. *Stress, 14*, 581–589. doi: 10.3109/10253890.2011.602146

Murgatroyd, C., & Spengler, D. (2012). Genetic variation in the epigenetic machinery and mental health. *Current Psychiatry Reports, 14*, 138–149. doi: 10.1007/s11920-012-0255-1

Murgatroyd, C., & Spengler, D. (2014). Polycomb binding precedes early-life stress responsive DNA methylation at the Avp enhancer. *PLoS One, 9*, e90277. doi: 10.1371/journal.pone.0090277

Okada, A., Ariizumi, M., & Okamoto, G. (1985). Study on the mechanism of the appearance of noise effects. *European Journal of Applied Phsiology, 53*, 364–367.

Pan, P., Fleming, A. S., Lawson, D., Jenkins, J. M., & McGowan, P. O. (2014). Within- and between-litter maternal care alter behavior and gene regulation in female offspring. *Behavioral Neuroscience, 128*, 736–748. doi: 10.1037/bne0000014

Pena, C. J., Neugut, Y. D., Calarco, C. A., & Champagne, F. A. (2014). Effects of maternal care on the development of midbrain dopamine pathways and reward-directed behavior in female offspring. *European Journal of Neuroscience, 39*, 946–956. doi: 10.1111/ejn.12479

Pickering, C., Gustafsson, L., Cebere, A., Nylander, I., & Liljequist, S. (2006). Repeated maternal separation of male Wistar rats alters glutamate receptor expression in the hippocampus but not the prefrontal cortex. *Brain Research, 1099*, 101–108. doi: 10.1016/j.brainres.2006.04.136

Plescia, F., Marino, R. A., Navarra, M., Gambino, G., Brancato, A., Sardo, P., & Cannizzaro, C. (2014). Early handling effect on female rat spatial and non-spatial learning and memory. *Behavioral Processes, 103*, 9–16. doi: 10.1016/j.beproc.2013.10.011

Plotsky, P. M., Thrivikraman, K. V., Nemeroff, C. B., Caldji, C., Sharma, S., & Meaney, M. J. (2005). Long-term consequences of neonatal rearing on central corticotropin-releasing factor systems in adult male rat offspring. *Neuropsychopharmacology, 30*, 2192–2204. doi: 10.1038/sj.npp.1300769

Roque, S., Mesquita, A. R., Palha, J. A., Sousa, N., & Correia-Neves, M. (2014). The behavioral and immunological impact of maternal separation: A matter of timing. *Frontiers in Behavioral Neuroscience, 8*, 192. doi: 10.3389/fnbeh.2014.00192

Sampedro-Piquero, P., Zancada-Menendez, C., Begega, A., Rubio, S., & Arias, J. L. (2013). Effects of environmental enrichment on anxiety responses, spatial memory and cytochrome c oxidase activity in adult rats. *Brain Research Bulletin, 98*, 1–9. doi: 10.1016/j.brainresbull.2013.06.006

Schroeder, M., Sultany, T., & Weller, A. (2013). Prenatal stress effects on emotion regulation differ by genotype and sex in prepubertal rats. *Developmental Psychobiology, 55*, 176–192. doi: 10.1002/dev.21010

Sequeira-Cordero, A., Masis-Calvo, M., Mora-Gallegos, A., & Fornaguera-Trias, J. (2013). Maternal behavior as an early modulator of neurobehavioral offspring responses by Sprague-Dawley rats. *Behavioural Brain Research, 237*, 63–70. doi: 10.1016/j.bbr.2012.09.028

Shoemaker, R., Wang, W., & Zhang, K. (2011). Mediators and dynamics of DNA methylation. *Wiley Interdisciplinary Reviews. Systems Biology and Medicine, 3*, 281–298. doi: 10.1002/wsbm.124

Skripuletz, T., Kruschinski, C., Pabst, R., von Horsten, S., & Stephan, M. (2010). Postnatal experiences influence the behavior in adult male and female Fischer and Lewis rats. *International Journal of Developmental Neuroscience, 28*, 561–571. doi: 10.1016/j.ijdevneu.2010.07.235

Suzuki, M. M., & Bird, A. (2008). DNA methylation landscapes: Provocative insights from epigenomics. *Nature Reviews: Genetics, 9*, 465–476. doi: 10.1038/nrg2341

Szyf, M. (2013). DNA methylation, behavior and early life adversity. *Journal of Genetics and Genomics, 40*, 331–338. doi: 10.1016/j.jgg.2013.06.004

Teperek-Tkacz, M., Pasque, V., Gentsch, G., & Ferguson-Smith, A. C. (2011). Epigenetic reprogramming: Is deamination key to active DNA demethylation? *Reproduction, 142*, 621–632. doi: 10.1530/REP-11-0148

Turecki, G., & Meaney, M. J. (2014). Effects of the social environment and stress on glucocorticoid receptor gene methylation: A systematic review. *Biological Psychiatry*. Advance online publication. doi: 10.1016/j.biopsych.2014.11.022

Tyrka, A. R., Parade, S. H., Price, L. H., Kao, H. T., Porton, B., Philip, N. S., … Carpenter, L. L. (2015). Alterations of mitochondrial DNA copy number and telomere length with early adversity and psychopathology. *Biological Psychiatry*. Advance online publication. doi: 10.1016/j.biopsych.2014.12.025

Vallee, M., Mayo, W., Dellu, F., Le Moal, M., Simon, H., & Maccari, S. (1997). Prenatal stress induces high anxiety and postnatal handling induces low anxiety in adult offspring: Correlation with stress-induced corticosterone secretion. *Journal of Neuroscience, 17*, 2626–2636.

Vallee, M., Mayo, W., Maccari, S., Le Moal, M., & Simon, H. (1996). Long-term effects of prenatal stress and handling on metabolic parameters: Relationship to corticosterone secretion response. *Brain Research, 712*, 287–292.

Van den Hove, D. L., Leibold, N. K., Strackx, E., Martinez-Claros, M., Lesch, K. P., Steinbusch, H. W., … Prickaerts, J. (2014). Prenatal stress and subsequent exposure to chronic mild stress in rats; interdependent effects on emotional behavior and the serotonergic system. *European Neuropsychopharmacology, 24*, 595–607. doi: 10.1016/j.euroneuro.2013.09.006

Veenema, A. H., Blume, A., Niederle, D., Buwalda, B., & Neumann, I. D. (2006). Effects of early life stress on adult malc aggression and hypothalamic vasopressin and serotonin. *European Journal of Neuroscience, 24*, 1711–1720. doi: 10.1111/j.1460-9568.2006.05045.x

Veenema, A. H., & Neumann, I. D. (2009). Maternal separation enhances offensive play-fighting, basal corticosterone and hypothalamic vasopressin mRNA expression in juvenile male rats. *Psychoneuroendocrinology, 34*, 463–467. doi: 10.1016/j.psyneuen.2008.10.017

Wang, A., Nie, W., Li, H., Hou, Y., Yu, Z., Fan, Q., & Sun, R. (2014). Epigenetic upregulation of corticotrophin-releasing hormone mediates postnatal maternal separation-induced memory deficiency. *PLoS One, 9*, e94394. doi: 10.1371/journal.pone.0094394

Weaver, I. C., Champagne, F. A., Brown, S. E., Dymov, S., Sharma, S., Meaney, M. J., & Szyf, M. (2005). Reversal of maternal programming of stress responses in adult offspring through methyl supplementation: Altering epigenetic marking later in life. *Journal of Neuroscience, 25*, 11045–11054. doi: 10.1523/JNEUROSCI.3652-05.2005

Weaver, I. C., La Plante, P., Weaver, S., Parent, A., Sharma, S., Diorio, J., … Meaney, M. J. (2001). Early environmental regulation of hippocampal glucocorticoid receptor gene expression: Characterization of intracellular mediators and potential genomic target sites. *Molecular and Cell Endocrinolgy, 185*, 205–218.

Weaver, I. C., Meaney, M. J., & Szyf, M. (2006). Maternal care effects on the hippocampal transcriptome and anxiety-mediated behaviors in the offspring that are reversible in adulthood. *Proceedings of the National Academy of Sciences of the United States of America, 103*, 3480–3485. doi: 10.1073/pnas.0507526103

Weinstock, M., Matlina, E., Maor, G. I., Rosen, H., & McEwen, B. S. (1992). Prenatal stress selectively alters the reactivity of the hypothalamic-pituitary adrenal system in the female rat. *Brain Research, 595*, 195–200.

Wilcoxon, J. S., & Redei, E. E. (2007). Maternal glucocorticoid deficit affects hypothalamic-pituitary-adrenal function and behavior of rat offspring. *Hormones and Behavior, 51*, 321–327. doi: 10.1016/j.yhbeh.2006.11.006

Yu, I. T., Lee, S. H., Lee, Y. S., & Son, H. (2004). Differential effects of corticosterone and dexamethasone on hippocampal neurogenesis in vitro. *Biochemical and Biophysical Research Communications, 317*, 484–490. doi: 10.1016/j.bbrc.2004.03.071

Zagron, G., & Weinstock, M. (2006). Maternal adrenal hormone secretion mediates behavioural alterations induced by prenatal stress in male and female rats. *Behavioral Brain Research, 175*, 323–328. doi: 10.1016/j.bbr.2006.09.003

Zohsel, K., Buchmann, A. F., Blomeyer, D., Hohm, E., Schmidt, M. H., Esser, G., … Laucht, M. (2014). Mothers' prenatal stress and their children's antisocial outcomes – a moderating role for the dopamine D4 receptor (DRD4) gene. *Journal of Child Psychology and Psychiatry, 55*, 69–76. doi: 10.1111/jcpp.12138

Margarete Bolten

University of Basel
Child and Adolescent Psychiatric Clinic
Schanzenstrasse 13
CH-4056 Basel
Switzerland
Tel. +41 (0) 61 265 89 60
Fax +41 (0) 61 265 89 61
E-mail margarete.bolten@upkbs.ch

From Animal Behavior to Human Health

An Animal-Assisted Mindfulness Intervention for Recurrent Depression

Elisabeth Schramm,[1,2] Karin Hediger,[3,4,5] and Undine E. Lang[2]

[1]Department of Psychiatry and Psychotherapy, University Medical Center Freiburg, Germany, [2]University Psychiatric Clinics (UPK), Basel, Switzerland, [3]Human and Animal Health Unit, Department of Epidemiology and Public Health, Swiss Tropical and Public Health Institute, Basel, Switzerland, [4]University of Basel, Switzerland, [5]IEMT Switzerland, Institute for Interdisciplinary Research on the Human-Animal Relationship, c/o Swiss TPH, Basel, Switzerland

Abstract. Animal-assisted therapy (AAT) has been shown to be effective in recent meta-analyses with an improvement of mental health, quality of life, and a decrease in the sense of isolation. Reduction of depressive symptoms in human beings is one of the most beneficial outcomes of AAT. For relapse prevention in depression, conventional mindfulness programs such as mindfulness-based cognitive therapy (MBCT) proved to be useful, but are often difficult to learn and produce high dropout rates in high risk patients. For this patient group, the teaching of mindfulness skills was facilitated by using sheep in an open pilot study. Six partially or unstable remitted patients with early trauma participated in eight group sessions of a nature and animal-assisted mindfulness training. The approach was feasible and highly accepted by participants with no dropouts. The results show a decrease of depressive symptoms and rumination, an improvement of overall mindfulness skills, but not of acceptance skills. Further studies using randomized controlled designs are warranted.

Keywords: animal-assisted therapy, depression, mindfulness

For centuries, animals were used to assist human beings with physically, mentally, or socially impaired functioning in various ways. This represents an important aspect of an integrative perspective of animal and human behavior and health referring to the One-Health concept (Hediger & Beetz, 2015; Zinsstag, Schelling, Waltner-Toews, Whittaker, & Tanner, 2015).

Animal-assisted therapy (AAT), as a form of animal-assisted interventions, is a "goal oriented, planned and structured therapeutic intervention" that focuses on "enhancing physical, cognitive, behavioral, and/or socio-emotional functioning of the human recipient" (International Association of Human-Animal Interaction Organizations, 2014). AAT is not defined as a homogeneous and independent form of intervention but serves as a method within the therapeutic process to facilitate the aspired goals.

In the last decade, a growing body of research has highlighted a multitude of positive effects of the human-animal interaction on human health and well-being. Moreover, research has pointed to underlying mechanisms that may explain how integrating animals in the therapeutic process can have additive positive effects (Beetz, Uvnäs-Moberg, Julius, & Kotrschal, 2012). Numerous studies indicate that the presence of an animal leads to reduced fear (e.g., Barker, Pandurangi, & Best, 2003; Cole, Gawlinski, Steers, & Kotlerman, 2007; Hoffmann et al., 2009; Lang, Jansen, Wertenauer, Gallinat, & Rapp, 2010), promotes calmness (Crowley-Robinson, Fenwick, & Blackshaw, 1996; Perkins, Bartlett, Travers, & Rand, 2008), and improves mood and prosocial behaviors (e.g., Banks & Banks, 2005; Colombo, Buono, Smania, Raviola, & De Leo, 2006; Marr et al., 2000; Nathans-Barel, Feldman, Berger, Modai, & Silver, 2005). Furthermore, interacting with animals is associated with stress buffering effects on a behavioral (Hansen, Messinger, Baun, & Megel, 1999) and physiological level (e.g., Beetz et al., 2011; Cole et al., 2007; Handlin et al., 2011; Odendaal & Meintjes, 2003). This is an often reproduced finding that can be even larger in the presence of a pet compared to the presence of a friend (Allen, Blascovich, & Mendes, 2002).

Although further research using higher quality randomized controlled trials is needed, AAT has been shown to be effective in recent systematic reviews and meta-analyses

DOI: 10.1027/2151-2604/a000220

(Kamioka et al., 2014; Nimer & Lundahl, 2007; Souter & Miller, 2007; Virués-Ortega, Pastor-Barriuso, Castellote, Población, & de Pedro-Cuesta, 2012). Nimer and Lundahl (2007) identified medium effect sizes in improving outcomes in the four areas of autism-spectrum symptoms, medical difficulties, behavioral problems, and emotional well-being. The authors conclude that integrating animals in therapy is a promising augmentation to established interventions. In another meta-analysis (Virués-Ortega et al., 2012), a large beneficial effect of AAT on social functioning, particularly in psychiatric patients, and moderate effects for depression, anxiety, and other behavioral disturbances were found. A newer systematic review confirms these findings (Kamioka et al., 2014) and concludes that AAT may have positive effects on mental and behavioral disorders such as depression, schizophrenia, and alcohol/drug addiction for people who like animals via the general improvement of mental health, elimination of the sense of isolation, and an improvement in quality of life (Kamioka et al., 2014). However, the authors state that the RCTs conducted have been of relatively low quality and were too heterogeneous to perform a meta-analysis.

Animal-Assisted Therapy (AAT) and Depression

One meta-analysis focused on depressive outcomes (Souter & Miller, 2007) and found a statistically significant, medium effect size for AAT and animal-assisted activities (AAA) in reducing depressive symptoms. In one study, however, no effect was found after 15 min of AAT in severely depressed patients before electroconvulsive treatment (Barker et al., 2003) which may be explained by the very short duration of exposure to the animal. Also, no effect of AAT on depressiveness, but on anxiety was found during a 12-week intervention in psychiatric patients with various diagnoses (only a small percentage with affective disorders) using farm animals (Berget, Ekeberg, Pedersen, & Braastad, 2011). However, in a study using a similar setting with clinically depressed patients, more patients in the intervention group experienced clinically significant changes in depression compared to a wait-list control group (Pedersen, Martinsen, Berget, & Braastad, 2012). Furthermore, in nursing home residents with dementia and depressive symptoms, an increase in depression over time was prevented if treatment-as-usual was combined with AAT in comparison to treatment as usual alone (Majić, Gutzmann, Heinz, Lang, & Rapp, 2013). Other studies found reduced depressive symptoms in residents of a long-term care facility (Le Roux & Kemp, 2009), older institutionalized adults without cognitive impairment (Colombo et al., 2006; Jessen, Cardiello, & Baun, 1996), and college students (Folse, Minder, Aycock, & Santana, 1994). In summary, existing studies give promising findings regarding the treatment of depression with animal-assisted therapy. Nevertheless, more research is needed in this area.

Efficacy Mechanisms of AAT

Different hypotheses are discussed as underlying mechanisms of the effects of AAT. Mostly discussed are the biophilia concept (Wilson, 1984), the social support hypothesis (McNicholas & Collis, 2006), and the attachment theory (Julius, Beetz, Kotrschal, Turner, & Uvnäs-Moberg, 2013). According to the biophilia concept (Wilson, 1984) human beings have an innate need to approach and interact with nature and nonhuman beings. As underlying psychobiological mechanisms of the effects of human-animal interaction, neurobiological processes are assumed. They seem to be mediated via the activation of the oxytocin system (see Beetz et al., 2012; Handlin et al., 2011; Julius et al., 2013; Nagasawa, Kikusui, Onaka, & Ohta, 2009; Odendaal & Meintjes, 2003).

On a psychosocial level, several more mechanisms may explain the effects of integrating animals in a therapeutic process which often has motivating effects or functions as "building a bridge" or an icebreaker (Wohlfarth, Mutschler, Beetz, Kreuser, & Korsten-Reck, 2013). An animal involves the patient in action and provides the opportunity for substitutional conversations and role switches. In addition, patients can experience themselves as a caregiver for a living being and receive close physical contact. Another central factor is the spontaneity that arises from animals in a therapy setting. Thus, patients have to adapt to new and unforeseen circumstances and have to stay "in the present." These mechanisms are facilitated by animals being nonjudgmental, communicating nonverbally, and providing prompt and authentic feedback.

For teaching mindfulness skills, animals are therefore particularly suitable since they have innate mindfulness skills themselves. They sense emotions and moods of human beings and react correspondingly (Olbrich, 2009). Animals are nonjudgmental and open-minded. This mirrors the attitude prompted in mindfulness like being present, nonjudgmental, accepting, open, and friendly. However, animals do not create a therapeutic process per se, but they rather support the change processes intended by the therapist (Fredrickson & Howie, 2000).

Depression and Mindfulness

Depressive disorders usually run a recurring course (Kessler et al., 2005; Kupfer, Frank, & Phillips, 2012). With every episode the risk of recurrence increases – after three episodes the risk is 90% (Eaton et al., 2008; Moffitt et al., 2010). Besides frequent episodes in the past, a high risk of relapse is also associated with an early onset and a history of early trauma which is prevalent in the majority of cases (Burcusa & Iacono, 2007). Prevention of relapse and recurrence thus represents one of the most important goals in the treatment of depression. Of the psychotherapy programs that have been designed specifically for the prevention of recurrent depression (Mindfulness-Based Cognitive Therapy/MBCT, Teasdale et al., 2000; Wellbeing Cognitive Therapy, Fava, Rafanelli, Grandi, Conti, &

Belluardo, 1998; Fava et al., 2004; Preventive Cognitive Therapy, Bockting, Hollon, Jarrett, Kuyken, & Dobson, 2005), MBCT is the best studied. MBCT combines methods of mindfulness-based stress reduction (MBSR; Kabat-Zinn, 1990) with concepts from cognitive behavioral therapy. Mindfulness is defined as a special form of paying attention – on purpose, in the present moment, and non-judgmentally (Kabat-Zinn, 1990). Mindfulness programs teach patients to maintain a moment-by-moment awareness of their thoughts, feelings, bodily sensations, and surrounding environment to prevent ruminating in the past or fearful thinking about the future.

Effectiveness of MBCT

A recent meta-analysis (Piet & Hougaard, 2011) based on seven clinical studies on relapse prevention in depression indicates that MBCT reduces relapse in patients with three or more episodes by 43% on average compared to treatment-as-usual (TAU). MBCT also proved to be equivalent to maintenance medication in preventing depressive relapses and recurrences in individuals at risk for relapse (Kuyken et al., 2015). A more recent meta-analysis of systematic reviews supports the use of MBSR and MBCT to alleviate symptoms, both mental and physical, in the adjunct treatment of cancer, cardiovascular disease, chronic pain, depression, anxiety disorders, and in prevention in healthy adults and children (Gotink et al., 2015). Accordingly, the method is recommended in international treatment guidelines for recurrent depression (e.g., National Institute for Health and Care Excellence, 2004).

Extension of the MBCT Program by Nature and Animal-Assisted Elements

It was shown that MBCT is particularly effective in patients highly at risk of relapse including more than two depressive episodes in the history, early interpersonal trauma, and unstable or partial remission (Bockting et al., 2015; Williams et al., 2014). For many patients with residual symptoms, in particular those with early traumatic experiences, the traditional practice of sitting meditations (which relates to the sole observation of breath or body sensations for a prolonged time period of 30–45 min) is difficult to learn and to endure in the sense of an exposure to one's own mind. A recent study (Michalak, Schultze, Heidenreich, & Schramm, in press) of 106 patients with persistent depressive symptoms, who were treated with either MBCT, the Cognitive Behavioral Analysis System of Psychotherapy (CBASP) or with TAU alone, yielded an unusually high dropout rate of 28% in the MBCT group. Clinical observation in the two centers in Freiburg and Bochum showed that many of the patients felt overwhelmed by the exercises that were part of the MBCT program (e.g., body scan, breathing space, sitting meditation, etc.). They prematurely terminated sessions, were emotionally agitated, or cried due to the intense focus on their inner state. Other MBCT studies also report high dropout rates (30% in Crane & Williams, 2010; ca. 20% in Segal et al., 2010; 25% in King et al., 2013), especially in the early stage of therapy (Crane & Williams, 2010; King et al., 2013). The investigation by King et al. (2013) on war veterans with chronic Posttraumatic Stress Disorder details that some of the patients who discontinued treatment prematurely reported an increased anxiety level during mindfulness and body-related exercises as the reason for termination. Other authors (e.g., Briere, Hodges, & Godbout, 2010) suggest possible contraindications for conventional mindfulness training in patients with reduced affect regulation and tolerance capacities. They recommend other, less activating options that are less direct and focus less on one's body or awareness of one's state of mind, such as Yoga or Loving-kindness exercises, and thereby permit a less overwhelming access to painful or upsetting memories or dysregulated experiences.

Like the MBCT program (Segal, Williams, & Teasdale, 2002), the modified nature and animal-assisted mindfulness training (NAMT) consists of eight weekly group sessions of 2.5 hr duration with a focus on the above-mentioned mindfulness techniques, psychoeducation regarding relapse prevention of depressive episodes, and the role of mindfulness and supportive-contemplative exchange of practice experiences in the group. The group concept included daily, formal (e.g., body scan using CDs), and informal exercises (e.g., mindfulness in everyday life while walking) and the 3-min breathing space. An overview of the session contents can be found in the Appendix.

The following modifications to the conventional MBCT program were made:

- Shortening of the mindfulness meditation exercises (in the sessions and as homework) from 45 min to 15–20 min, shortening of the body scan exercises to a maximum of 15 min.
- The "raisin exercise" is conducted with mindfully collected objects from nature (e.g., daisies, strawberries, chestnuts, etc.).
- Exercises for mindful observing, describing, and participating are conducted with natural materials (e.g., building stone towers) or animals (e.g., brushing or leading animals) and in nature (barefoot walking meditation, eye scan, and hearing meditation in nature).
- Mindfulness in everyday life is based on the natural life (e.g., cleaning enclosures, collecting herbs, walking with the sheep in the herd, sheering and wool processing).
- Compassion and self-compassion with animals.

Open Pilot Study

We evaluated the feasibility, acceptability, and effectiveness of the above-described NAMT program in an open pilot study on patients with partially or unstable remitted major depressive disorder after response to antidepressants and psychotherapy. Other inclusion criteria were an age between

18 and 70 years, patients had to be in psychiatric care and signed the informed consent. Exclusion criteria were acute suicidality and another acute primary psychiatric disorder.

Six patients aged 21–64 years ($M = 47.67$ years; $SD = 16.06$ years) were included. All patients were on stable antidepressant medication for at least 3 weeks before the beginning of the program and all reported early trauma in their prior history.

The NAMT group program was conducted by a registered psychotherapist (E. Sch) with comprehensive training in mindfulness as well as extensive experience with depression treatment and educational work with the sheep participating in the study. The program was accompanied by an animal caretaker from Mundenhof (animal farm run by the city of Freiburg, Germany). Eight "Coburger fox-sheep," a breed of *Ovis gmelini aries*, participated in the program. They are familiar with interacting with human beings and trained to walk on the leash. The animals' stress levels during the meetings were continuously monitored by the animal caretaker participating in the program. No signs of stress (e.g., restlessness, frequent urination, accelerated breathing, etc.) were detected in the animals, but – on the contrary – they actively sought contact with the participants. All training sessions took place outside at the Mundenhof farm.

As the primary outcome served the change in depressive symptoms as rated by the patients by means of the Beck Depression Inventory (BDI-II). Secondary outcomes were rumination using the Response Style Questionnaire (RSQ), a scale with the dimensions "Rumination," "Distraction" (behavioral and cognitive distraction from negative mood), and "Negative thoughts about oneself." In addition, mindfulness skills were assessed applying the German version of the Kentucky Inventory of Mindfulness Skills (KIMS-D) and the Freiburg Mindfulness Questionnaire (FFA). In the KIMS-D, four dimensions are distinguished: "Observing" (attentive perception of external and internal stimuli such as bodily sensations, cognitions, emotions, sounds, or smells), "Describing," "Acting with awareness" (participation – engaging entirely in an activity) and "Accepting without judgment" (allow reality as it is, without avoidance, change, or escape). In addition, participant satisfaction was evaluated by means of a self-developed change questionnaire. Remission was – similar to other studies – defined as a BDI value of less than 10 points.

Due to the small sample size the statistical analysis was carried out using the nonparametric Wilcoxon signed-rank test for dependent samples. The sum or dimension values of the questionnaires completed at the beginning of the 8-week NAMT were compared with those after completion. The level of significance was 0.05.

Results

None of the patients dropped out of the group program, all patients participated fully in all meetings. Figure 1 shows

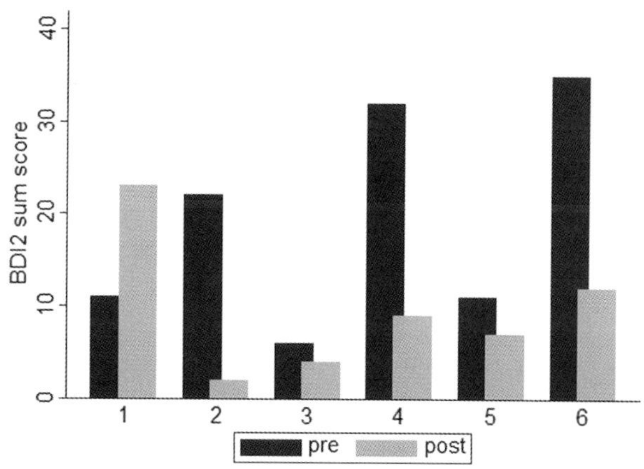

Figure 1. Total scores on the BDI-II before (pre) and after the eight week intervention (post). The numbers from 1 to 6 represent the six participants.

that on the BDI-II, five of the six patients improved in depressive symptoms after the intervention (by an average of 10.0 points). Four of the six patients were, with a BDI score of less than 10, in the range of remission, compared to only one patient at the beginning of the program. Overall, no significant increase in BDI-II scores from baseline to post-measurement occurred (see Table 1).

"Rumination" and "Negative thoughts about oneself" significantly decreased after the intervention, "Distraction" improved on average, however not significantly (see Table 1). Scores on the total scale of the KIMS-D improved significantly by the end of treatment (see Table 1). Among the four dimensions, "Observing" and "Acting with awareness" significantly improved. No improvement was found for "Accepting without judgment" and "Describing." General mindfulness skills measured by the FFA significantly increased after treatment (see Table 1).

Summary and Conclusions

The findings show that a nature and animal-assisted mindfulness training was feasible and highly accepted by the patients. All patients attended all sessions and were compliant with the homework. In addition, there were no dropouts. NAMT may therefore represent an effective new approach for unstable remitted and early traumatized patients. Overall, the patients reported after the program being more attentive, perceiving situations mindfully without simultaneously evaluating them, and having learned from nature how to better deal with problems.

After 8 weeks, the intervention led on average to a further stabilization or improvement in depressive symptoms. The tendency to ruminate declined significantly. General mindfulness skills and in particular the skills of "Observing" and "Acting with awareness" increased significantly. Least improved, possibly due to the short duration of therapy, was the capacity for acceptance, especially of

Table 1. Pre- and post-values of the different measures: BDI-II = Beck Depression Inventory; RSQ = Response Style Questionnaire; KIMS-D = Kentucky Inventory of Mindfulness Skills; FFA = Freiburg Mindfulness Questionnaire

Measure	Scales	Time	*M*	*SD*	*Z*	*p*	ϕ
BDI-II		Pre	19.5	12.08	1.577	.155	0.644
		Post	9.5	7.5			
RSQ	Rumination	Pre	54.0	8.97	2.023	.043	0.826
		Post	39.2	10.38			
	Distraction	Pre	21.6	6.31	1.361	.174	0.556
		Post	23.8	7.85			
	Negative thoughts about yourself	Pre	11.6	2.61	2.032	.042	0.830
		Post	8.0	2.55			
KIMS-D	Total	Pre	119.6	7.57	2.023	.043	0.826
		Post	151.2	18.57			
	Observing	Pre	36.2	10.66	2.023	.043	0.826
		Post	48.8	5.54			
	Acting with awareness	Pre	25.4	7.01	2.023	.043	0.827
		Post	32.8	4.98			
	Accepting without judgment	Pre	27.0	11.05	1.219	.222	0.498
		Post	34.8	8.38			
	Describing	Pre	31.0	6.28	1.753	.080	0.716
		Post	34.8	4.92			
FFA		Pre	27.67	5.99	2.207	.027	0.901
		Post	40.83	7.78			

unpleasant things. Consequently, the acceptance module will be extended and supplemented by additional exercises (e.g., acceptance of negative phenomena in nature).

Despite limitations such as a small sample, no control group, and the inclusion of only participants who like animals, the preliminary results of this pilot study are encouraging and warrant further investigation of the NAMT in a larger, randomized sample of patients with high-risk for relapse. The exercises within the NAMT are easy to apply in an efficient group format. The modified mindfulness program in nature provides an alternative strategy that may also be used for patients who react with increased arousal, anxiety, or feeling overwhelmed by the conventional practice of mindfulness.

Acknowledgments

We thank Angelika Fischhaber and Nina Grimm for their contributions to the program and the Mundenhof, Freiburg, Germany for the cooperation.

References

Allen, K., Blascovich, J., & Mendes, W. B. (2002). Cardiovascular reactivity and the presence of pets, friends, and spouses: The truth about cats and dogs. *Psychosomatic Medicine, 64*, 727–739. doi: 10.1097/01.PSY.0000024236.11538.41

Banks, M. R., & Banks, W. A. (2005). The effects of animal-assisted therapy on loneliness in an elderly population in long-term care facilities. *Anthrozoös, 18*, 396–408. doi: 10.2752/089279305785593983

Barker, S. B., Pandurangi, A. K., & Best, A. M. (2003). Effects of animal-assisted therapy on patients' anxiety, fear, and depression before ECT. *Journal of ECT, 19*, 38–44. doi: 10.1097/00124509-200303000-00008

Beetz, A., Kotrschal, K., Turner, D. C., Hediger, K., Uvnäs-Moberg, K., & Julius, H. (2011). The effect of a real dog, toy dog and friendly person on insecurely attached children during a stressful task: An exploratory study. *Anthrozoös, 24*, 349–368. doi: 10.2752/175303711X13159027359746

Beetz, A., Uvnäs-Moberg, K., Julius, H., & Kotrschal, K. (2012). Psychosocial and psychophysiological effects of human-animal interactions: The possible role of oxytocin. *Frontiers in Psychology, 3*, 234. doi: 10.3389/fpsyg.2012.00234

Berget, B., Ekeberg, Ø., Pedersen, I., & Braastad, B. O. (2011). Animal-assisted therapy with farm animals for persons with psychiatric disorders: Effects on anxiety and depression, a randomized controlled trial. *Occupational Therapy in Mental Health, 27*, 50–64. doi: 10.1080/0164212X.2011.543641

Bockting, C. L., Hollon, S. D., Jarrett, R. B., Kuyken, W., & Dobson, K. (2015). A lifetime approach to major depressive disorder: The contributions of psychological interventions in preventing relapse and recurrence. *Clinical Psychology Review.* Advance online publication. doi: 10.1016/j.cpr.2015.02.003

Bockting, C. L., Schene, A. H., Spinhoven, P., Koeter, M. W., Wouters, L. F., Huyser, J., & Kamphuis, J. H. (2005). Preventing relapse/recurrence in recurrent depression with cognitive therapy: A randomized controlled trial. *Journal of Consulting and Clinical Psychology, 73*, 647–657. doi: 10.1037/0022-006X.73.4.647

Briere, J., Hodges, M., & Godbout, N. (2010). Traumatic stress, affect dysregulation, and dysfunctional avoidance: A structural equation model. *Journal of Traumatic Stress, 23*, 767–774. doi: 10.1002/jts.20578

Burcusa, S. L., & Iacono, W. G. (2007). Risk for recurrence in depression. *Clinical Psychology Review, 27*, 959–985. doi: 10.1016/j.cpr.2007.02.005

Cole, K. M., Gawlinski, A., Steers, N., & Kotlerman, J. (2007). Animal-assisted therapy in patients hospitalized with heart failure. *American Journal of Critical Care, 16*, 575–585.

Colombo, G., Buono, M. D., Smania, K., Raviola, R., & De Leo, D. (2006). Pet therapy and institutionalized elderly: A study on 144 cognitively unimpaired subjects. *Archives of Gerontology and Geriatrics, 42*, 207–216. doi: 10.1016/j.archger.2005.06.011

Crane, C., & Williams, J. M. (2010). Factors associated with attrition from mindfulness-based cognitive therapy in patients with a history of suicidal depression. *Mindfulness, 1*, 10–20. doi: 10.1007/s12671-010-0003-8

Crowley-Robinson, P., Fenwick, D. C., & Blackshaw, J. K. (1996). A long-term study of elderly people in nursing homes with visiting and resident dogs. *Applied Animal Behaviour Science, 47*, 137–148. doi: 10.1016/0168-1591(95)01017-3

Eaton, W. W., Shao, H., Nestadt, G., Lee, H. B., Bienvenu, O. J., & Zandi, P. (2008). Population-based study of first onset and chronicity in major depressive disorder. *Archives of General Psychiatry, 65*, 513–520. doi: 10.1001/archpsyc.65.5.513

Fava, G. A., Rafanelli, C., Grandi, S., Conti, S., & Belluardo, P. (1998). Prevention of recurrent depression with cognitive behavioral therapy: Preliminary findings. *Archives of General Psychiatry, 55*, 816–820. doi: 10.1001/archpsyc.55.9.816

Fava, G. A., Ruini, C., Rafanelli, C., Finos, L., Conti, S., & Grandi, S. (2004). Six-year outcome of cognitive behavior therapy for prevention of recurrent depression. *American Journal of Psychiatry, 161*, 1872–1876. doi: 10.1176/appi.ajp.161.10.1872

Folse, E. B., Minder, C. C., Aycock, M. J., & Santana, R. T. (1994). Animal-assisted therapy and depression in adult college students. *Anthrozoös, 7*, 188–194. doi: 10.2752/089279394787001880

Fredrickson, M., & Howie, A. R. (2000). Methods, standards, guidelines, and considerations in selecting animals for animal-assisted therapy. Part B: Guidelines and standards for animal selection in animal-assisted activity and therapy programs. In A. H. Fine (Ed.), *Handbook on animal-assisted therapy: Theoretical foundations and guidelines for practice* (pp. 99–114). San Diego, CA: Academic Press.

Gotink, R. A., Chu, P., Busschbach, J. J. V., Benson, H., Fricchione, G. L., & Hunink, M. G. M. (2015). Standardised mindfulness-based interventions in healthcare: An overview of systematic reviews and meta-analyses of RCTs. *PLoS One, 10*, e0124344. doi: 10.1371/journal.pone.0124344

Handlin, L., Hydbring-Sandberg, E., Nilsson, A., Ejdebäck, M., Jansson, A., & Uvnäs-Moberg, K. (2011). Short-term interaction between dogs and their owners: Effects on oxytocin, cortisol, insulin and heart rate – an exploratory study. *Anthrozoös, 24*, 301–315. doi: 10.2752/175303711X13045914865385

Hansen, K. M., Messinger, C. J., Baun, M. M., & Megel, M. (1999). Companion animals alleviating distress in children. *Anthrozoös, 12*, 142–148. doi: 10.2752/089279399787000264

Hediger, K., & Beetz, A. (2015). The role of human-animal interaction in education. In J. Zinsstag, E. Schelling, D. Waltner-Toews, M. Whittaker, & M. Tanner (Eds.), *One Health: The theory and practice of integrated health approaches* (pp. 73–84). Wallingford, UK: CABI Publishing.

Hoffmann, A. O. M., Lee, A. H., Wertenauer, F., Ricken, R., Jansen, J. J., Gallinat, J., & Lang, U. E. (2009). Dog-assisted intervention significantly reduces anxiety in hospitalized patients with major depression. *European Journal of Integrative Medicine, 1*, 145–148. doi: 10.1016/j.eujim.2009.08.002

International Association of Human-Animal Interaction Organizations. (2014). *IAHAIO White Paper. The IAHAIO definitions for animal assisted intervention and guidelines for wellness of animals involved*. Retrieved from http://www.iahaio.org/new/fileuploads/4163IAHAIO%20WHITE%20PAPER-%20FINAL%20-%20NOV%2024-2014.pdf

Jessen, J., Cardiello, F., & Baun, M. M. (1996). Avian companionship in alleviation of depression, loneliness, and low morale of older adults in skilled rehabilitation units. *Psychological Reports, 78*, 339–348. doi: 10.2466/pr0.1996.78.1.339

Julius, H., Beetz, A., Kotrschal, K., Turner, D. C., & Uvnäs-Moberg, K. (2013). *Attachment to pets: An integrative view of human-animal relationships with implications for therapeutic practice*. Göttingen, Germany: Hogrefe.

Kabat-Zinn, J. (1990). *Full catastrophe living: Using the wisdom of your body and mind to face stress, pain, and illness*. New York, NY: Delacorte Press.

Kamioka, H., Okada, S., Tsutani, K., Park, H., Okuizumi, H., Handa, S., ... Mutoh, Y. (2014). Effectiveness of animal-assisted therapy: A systematic review of randomized controlled trials. *Complementary Therapies in Medicine, 22*, 371–390. doi: 10.1016/j.ctim.2013.12.016

Kessler, R. C., Berglund, P., Demler, O., Jin, R., Merikangas, K. R., & Walters, E. E. (2005). Lifetime prevalence and age-of-onset distributions of DSM-IV disorders in the National Comorbidity Survey Replication. *Archives of General Psychiatry, 62*, 593–602. doi: 10.1001/archpsyc.62.6.593

King, A. P., Erickson, T. M., Giardino, N. D., Favorite, T., Rauch, S. A., Robinson, E., ... Liberzon, , I. (2013). A pilot study of group mindfulness-based cognitive therapy (MBCT) for combat veterans with posttraumatic stress disorder (PTSD). *Depression and Anxiety, 30*, 638–645. doi: 10.1002/da.22104

Kupfer, D. J., Frank, E., & Phillips, M. L. (2012). Major depressive disorder: New clinical, neurobiological, and treatment perspectives. *Lancet, 379*, 1045–1055. doi: 10.1016/S0140-6736(11)60602-8

Kuyken, W., Hayes, R., Barrett, B., Byng, R., Dalgleish, D., Kessler, D., ... Byford, S. (2015). Effectiveness and cost-effectiveness of mindfulness-based cognitive therapy compared with maintenance antidepressant treatment in the prevention of depressive relapse or recurrence (PREVENT): A randomised controlled trial. *Lancet, 386*, 63–73. doi: 10.1016/S0140-6736(14)62222-4

Lang, U. E., Jansen, J. B., Wertenauer, F., Gallinat, J., & Rapp, M. A. (2010). Reduced anxiety during dog assisted interviews in acute schizophrenic patients. *European Journal of Integrative Medicine, 2*, 123–127. doi: 10.1016/j.eujim.2010.07.002

Le Roux, M. C., & Kemp, R. (2009). Effect of a companion dog on depression and anxiety levels of elderly residents in a long-term care facility. *Psychogeriatrics, 9*, 23–26. doi: 10.1111/j.1479-8301.2009.00268.x

Majić, T., Gutzmann, H., Heinz, A., Lang, U. E., & Rapp, M. A. (2013). Animal-assisted therapy and agitation and depression in nursing home residents with dementia: A matched case-control trial. *American Journal of Geriatric Psychiatry, 21*, 1052–1059. doi: 10.1016/j.jagp.2013.03.004

Marr, C. A., French, L., Thompson, D., Drum, L., Greening, G., Mormon, J., ... Hughes, C. W. (2000). Animal-assisted therapy in psychiatric rehabilitation. *Anthrozoös, 13*, 43–47. doi: 10.2752/089279300786999950

McNicholas, J., & Collis, G. M. (2006). Animal as social supports: Insights for understanding animal-assisted therapy. In A. H. Fine (Ed.), *Handbook on animal-assisted therapy: Theoretical foundations and guidelines for practice* (2nd ed., pp. 49–71). San Diego, CA: Academic Press.

Michalak, J., Schultze, M., Heidenreich, T., & Schramm, E. (in press). Mindfulness-based cognitive therapy vs. cognitive behavioral analysis system of psychotherapy for chronically depressed patients: A randomized controlled trial. *Journal of Consulting and Clinical Psychology*.

Moffitt, T. E., Caspi, A., Taylor, A., Kokaua, J., Milne, B. J., Polanczyk, G., & Poulton, R. (2010). How common are common mental disorders? Evidence that lifetime prevalence rates are doubled by prospective versus retrospective ascertainment. *Psychological Medicine, 40*, 899–909. doi: 10.1017/S0033291709991036

Nagasawa, M., Kikusui, T., Onaka, T., & Ohta, M. (2009). Dog's gaze at its owner increases owner's urinary oxytocin during social interaction. *Hormones and Behavior, 55*, 434–441. doi: 10.1016/j.yhbeh.2008.12.002

Nathans-Barel, I., Feldman, P., Berger, B., Modai, I., & Silver, H. (2005). Animal-assisted therapy ameliorates anhedonia in schizophrenia patients. A controlled pilot study. *Psychotherapy and Psychosomatics, 74*, 31–35. doi: 10.1159/000082024

National Institute for Health and Care Excellence. (2004). *Depression: Management of depression in primary and secondary care. NICE Clinical Guideline 23*. Retrieved from http://www.nice.org.uk/guidance/cg23

Nimer, J., & Lundahl, B. (2007). Animal-assisted therapy: A meta-analysis. *Anthrozoös, 20*, 225–238. doi: 10.2752/089279307X224773

Odendaal, J. S. J., & Meintjes, R. A. (2003). Neurophysiological correlates of affiliative behaviour between humans and dogs. *Veterinary Journal, 165*, 296–301. doi: 10.1016/S1090-0233(02)00237-X

Olbrich, E. (2009). Mensch-Tier-Beziehungen. In K. Lenz & F. Nestmann (Eds.), *Handbuch Persönliche Beziehungen* [Handbook of personal relationships] (pp. 353–379). Weinheim, Germany: Beltz Juventa.

Pedersen, I., Martinsen, E. W., Berget, B., & Braastad, B. O. (2012). Farm animal-assisted intervention for people with clinical depression: A randomized controlled trial. *Anthrozoös, 25*, 149–160. doi: 10.2752/175303712X13316289505260

Perkins, J., Bartlett, H., Travers, C., & Rand, J. (2008). Dog-assisted therapy for older people with dementia: A review. *Australasian Journal on Ageing, 27*, 177–182. doi: 10.1111/j.1741-6612.2008.00317.x

Piet, J., & Hougaard, E. (2011). The effect of mindfulness-based cognitive therapy for prevention of relapse in recurrent major depressive disorder: A systematic review and meta-analysis. *Clinical Psychology Review, 31*, 1032–1040. doi: 10.1016/j.cpr.2011.05.002

Segal, Z. V., Bieling, P., Young, T., MacQueen, G., Cooke, R., Martin, L., ... Levitan, R. D. (2010). Antidepressant monotherapy vs sequential pharmacotherapy and mindfulness-based cognitive therapy, or placebo, for relapse prophylaxis in recurrent depression. *Archives of General Psychiatry, 67*, 1256–1264. doi: 10.1001/archgenpsychiatry.2010.168

Segal, Z. V., Williams, J. M. G., & Teasdale, J. D. (2002). *Mindfulness-based cognitive therapy for depression: A new approach to preventing relapse*. New York, NY: Guilford Press.

Souter, M. A., & Miller, M. D. (2007). Do animal-assisted activities effectively treat depression? A meta-analysis. *Anthrozoös, 20*, 167–180. doi: 10.2752/175303707X207954

Teasdale, J. D., Segal, Z. V., Williams, J. M., Ridgeway, V. A., Soulsby, J. M., & Lau, M. A. (2000). Prevention of relapse/recurrence in major depression by mindfulness-based cognitive therapy. *Journal of Consulting and Clinical Psychology, 68*, 615–623. doi: 10.1037/0022-006X.68.4.615

Virués-Ortega, J., Pastor-Barriuso, R., Castellote, J. M., Población, A., & de Pedro-Cuesta, J. (2012). Effect of animal-assisted therapy on the psychological and functional status of elderly populations and patients with psychiatric disorders: A meta-analysis. *Health Psychology Review, 6*, 197–221. doi: 10.1080/17437199.2010.534965

Williams, J. M., Crane, C., Barnhofer, T., Brennan, K., Duggan, D. S., Fennell, M. J., ... Russell, I. T. (2014). Mindfulness-based cognitive therapy for preventing relapse in recurrent depression: A randomized dismantling trial. *Journal of Consulting and Clinical Psychology, 82*, 275–286. doi: 10.1037/a0035036

Wilson, E. O. (1984). *Biophilia*. Cambridge, MA: Harvard University Press.

Wohlfarth, R., Mutschler, B., Beetz, A., Kreuser, F., & Korsten-Reck, U. (2013). Dogs motivate obese children for physical activity: Key elements of a motivational theory of animal-assisted interventions. *Frontiers in Psychology, 4*, 796. doi: 10.3389/fpsyg.2013.00796

Zinsstag, J., Schelling, E., Waltner-Toews, D., Whittaker, M., & Tanner, M. (Eds.). (2015). *One Health: The theory and practice of integrated health approaches*. Wallingford, UK: CABI Publishing.

Elisabeth Schramm

Universitäre Psychiatrische Kliniken (UPK)
Wilhelm-Klein-Str. 27
CH-4012 Basel
Switzerland
Tel. +41 613 255 206
Fax +41 613 255 518
E-mail Elisabeth.Schramm@upkbs.ch

Appendix

Session number	Theme	Content
1	Mindfully observing and describing in nature	– *Overview of the program, psychoeducation* (on relapse prevention of depressive episodes, the role of mindfulness, and the rationale of NAMT) – *Introduction exercise on mindfully observing* (modified raisin exercise) – *Mindfully observing, describing, and participating with sheep* (in silence: learn to describe and differentiate the sheep from each other, mindfully approaching and mimicking the sheep, brush or caress sheep with each half attention on yourself and on the animal) – *Contemplation/exchange, 3-minute breathing space, homework*
2	Mindfulness in nature everyday life, being present	– *3-minute breathing space* (dealing with obstacles) – Review of homework – *Mindfulness in nature everyday life* (in silence: cleaning pen, be present, flow experience, being vs. doing mindfulness) – *Mindfully leading sheep* (in silence: pick, approach and leash animal, lead the animal outside the pen using breathing to get aligned with yourself and in sync with the animal, be present) – *Contemplation/exchange, body scan, homework*
3	Mindfully participating in nature	– *Body scan* – Review of homework – *Mindfully leading sheep* (in silence: unleash the sheep outside the pen, observe and describe what they are eating, mindful walking with the sheep on different underground, find your place in the herd, be part of the herd) – *Eye scan in nature* – *Contemplation/exchange, 3-minute breathing space, homework*
4	Compassion	– *Introduction in meta-meditation with exercise* (compassion) – Review of homework – *Compassion with the animal* (in silence: pick a sheep that attracts you least, loving-kindness exercise with the sheep) – *Contemplation/exchange, 3-minute breathing space, homework*
5	Self-compassion	– *Self-compassion exercise* – Review of homework – *Self-compassion in nature* (in silence: pick a meditation place in nature that has a positive impact on you) – *In pairs of two: Collect energy spender in nature that can be integrated in your everyday life* – *Contemplation/exchange, body scan, homework*
6	Acceptance without judgment	– *Mountain meditation* – Review of homework – *Introduction into an accepting attitude in mindfulness, examples from nature/sheep* – *Find-balance-and-acceptance exercise, letting go for a fresh beginning* (in silence: build a stone tower while breathing mindfully) – *Mindfully leading and being led by sheep* (in silence: get in sync with animal and switch leading and being led, letting go of own agenda) – *Contemplation/exchange, 3-minute breathing space, homework*

(Continued on next page)

Appendix (Continued)

Session number	Theme	Content
7	Participating in nature, dealing with negative feelings and thoughts	– *Acceptance meditation exercise* (dealing with negative feelings and thoughts) – Review of homework – *Mindfully participating in processing of natural material* (e.g., sheering sheep, washing and combing their wool, felting or yarning, etc., getting into flow, getting whole, accepting nature's rules) – *Hearing meditation in nature* (dealing with negative feelings and thoughts) – *Contemplation/exchange, 3-minute breathing space, homework*
8	Integration	– *Sitting meditation* – Review of homework – *Integration nature, self and mindfulness* (being present) – *Gratefulness exercise* – *Contemplation/exchange, 3-minute breathing space*

Call for Papers

"Neuroscience and Education: Added Value of Combining Brain Imaging and Behavioral Research"

A Topical Issue of the *Zeitschrift für Psychologie*

Guest Editors: Elsbeth Stern (ETH Zürich, Switzerland),
Roland H. Grabner (University of Graz, Austria),
and Ralph Schumacher (ETH Zürich, Switzerland)

Educational Neuroscience has emerged as an interdisciplinary field, mainly stimulated by the improvement of brain imaging techniques and a growing interest in human learning inside and outside of schools. Getting information about human learning and cognition beyond behavioral observation by recording brain characteristics was highly appreciated by many learning researchers. At the same time, however, they were concerned about the uncritical enthusiasm and unrealistic expectations among many parents, teachers, and policy makers. In many countries, this was spurred by some representatives from neuroscience who attempted to use insights from basic brain research for school reforms and improving classroom practice. Meaningless slogans like "brain-based learning" got attention while at the same time sound scientific insights about school-related learning from behavioral research were ignored. This said, however, does not mean to underestimate the added value of including insights from neuroscience in research on learning and instruction.

A decade ago, the guest editors of this topical issue were invited by the German Federal Ministry of Education and Research to write an expert report on "Educational Research and the Neurosciences: Expectations, Evidence, and Research prospects." The German version appeared in 2005, and the English translation was published 1 year later (http://www.ifvll.ethz.ch/research/bildungsreform_band13_en.pdf).

The report was based on contributions and discussions of an interdisciplinary workshop with psychologists, educational researchers, and neuroscientists. The focus was on the bidirectional relationship between neuroscience and behavioral research: On the one hand, research questions on school-related learning were discussed which can be informed by neuroscience. On the other hand, it was realized that the best way to learn more about what makes the human brain unique is observing it during educational activities.

Following the expert report, the German Ministry launched the research initiative NIL (Neuroscience, Instruction, Learning), and similar initiatives have been emerging in many other countries. Therefore, time has come for looking back to the scientific progress made in the past decade. In the final chapter of the expert report, the guest editors raised several topics worth being addressed in forthcoming research. In the present topical issue we would like to document the progress that has been made in the past decade. Therefore articles dealing with the following topics are welcome:

1) Deviant brain functions in children who suffer from dyslexia or dyscalculia: To what extent have insights from neuroscience informed the development of therapeutic treatments?
2) Effects of training on brain functions: It is heavily debated whether certain kinds of training can improve general brain functioning and thereby foster remote transfer. Training studies which considered brain imaging data are therefore welcome.
3) Individual differences in brain functioning: Neural efficiency has been identified as a brain correlate of intelligence. Studies on the interaction of intelligence and prior knowledge in information processing and learning are appreciated.
4) Neural underpinnings of error processing: As learning almost inevitably goes with making errors, new insights into feedback and error correction mechanisms can be presented.

DOI: 10.1027/2151-2604/a000213

5) The emergence of insights: The acquisition of complex and meaningful content knowledge is an arduous and time-consuming process. Insights often appear all of a sudden, although severe changes on the knowledge base must have taken place before. Finding neural indicators of successful learning trajectories before behavior/achievement is visible is a particularly worthwhile question.
6) Cognitive load: Successful problem solving depends on an efficient use of working memory capacity. Research on how the reduction of extraneous load in presenting learning material affects brain functioning is appreciated.
7) Effects of modalities: In formal domains like science and mathematics, many problems can be presented and processed in spatial or in symbolic modalities. Progress made in identifying neural correlates of these representations and their relationship to achievement fit the topical issue.

How to submit: Interested authors should submit a letter of intent including: (1) a working title for the manuscript, (2) names, affiliations, and contact information for all authors, and (3) an abstract of no more than 500 words detailing the content of the proposed manuscript to Elsbeth Stern (stern@ifv.gess.ethz.ch).

There is a two-stage submissions process. Initially, interested authors are requested to submit only abstracts of their proposed papers. Authors of the selected abstracts will then be invited to submit full papers. All papers will undergo blind peer review.

Deadline for submission of abstracts is October 31, 2015.

Deadline for submission of full papers is February 29, 2016.

The journal seeks to maintain a short turnaround time, with the final version of the accepted papers being due by May 15, 2016. The topical issue will be published as issue 4 (2016).

For additional information, please contact any of the guest editors.

About the Journal

The *Zeitschrift für Psychologie*, founded in 1890, is the oldest psychology journal in Europe and the second oldest in the world. One of the founding editors was Hermann Ebbinghaus. Since 2007 it is published in English and devoted to publishing topical issues that provide state-of-the-art reviews of current research in psychology.

Guidelines for Article Preparation

- Only English-language submissions can be considered.
- Contributions must be original (not published previously or currently under review for publication elsewhere).
- Review and original articles should not exceed 45,000 characters and spaces in length, including references, figures, and tables (allowances for figures and tables should be deducted on the basis of size – approximately 1,250 characters for a quarter-page figure/table).
- Other submission formats (research summaries, opinion pieces, etc.) may be considered, please contact the editors for details.
- Reference citations in the text and in the reference list should be in accordance with the principles set out in the *Publication Manual of the American Psychological Association* (6th ed.) – see also any recent issue of the journal.

For detailed author guidelines, please see the journal's website at www.hogrefe.com/journals/zfp/

Sample pages at www.hogrefe.com!

Henri Julius, Andrea Beetz, Kurt Kotrschal, Dennis Turner, & Kerstin Uvnäs-Moberg

Attachment to Pets

An Integrative View of Human-Animal Relationships with Implications for Therapeutic Practice

2013, xiv + 192 pp. with Forewords by Judith Solomon and Sir Patrick Bateson
ISBN 978-0-88937-442-3,
US $49.00 / £ 27.90 / € 34.95

"A comprehensive, scientific foundation for human-animal therapy." **(Judith Solomon)**

In recent years, the ancient symbiosis between humans and their pets has entered a new phase, marked by the burgeoning clinical specialty of human-animal therapy. This approach uses the relationship between humans and their (mainly) mammalian pets to support the growth of emotion regulation, social skills, and mental health in children, adolescents, and adults.

But how are humans and animals able to develop close bonds at all? What makes it possible for animals to have a therapeutic effect on humans? And how can we best use this understanding in animal-assisted therapy?

In this unique book, a team of expert biologists and psychologists integrate and combine sophisticated biological and psychological knowledge to answer these questions. Together they have created a comprehensive, scientific foundation for human-animal therapy, a foundation that will facilitate the development, implementation, and evaluation of effective new interventions.

Praise for the Book:

"The authors accomplish a long-awaited merging of evolutionary, biophysiological, and psychological processes likely to occur in human-animal interaction in an intellectually stimulating and practically applicable narrative. This book is useful for students, scientists, and practitioners, and will be essential to guide advancement of the field of human-animal interaction."
Rebecca Johnson, PhD, RN, FAAN, President, International Association of Human–Animal Interaction Organizations, Professor & Director, Research Center for Human–Animal Interaction, MU College of Veterinary Medicine, Columbia, MO

"This much-needed integrative book explains how the relationship between animals and therapists/clients can effectively be used to provide animal-assisted interventions with positive outcomes. It also presents a valuable scholarly framework that advances the endeavors of the International Society for Animal-Assisted Therapy."
Lynette Hart, PhD, School of Veterinary Medicine, University of California, Davis, CA

Hogrefe Publishing
30 Amberwood Parkway · Ashland, OH 44805 · USA
Tel: (800) 228-3749 · Fax: (419) 281-6883
E-Mail: customerservice@hogrefe.com

Hogrefe Publishing
Merkelstr. 3· 37085 Göttingen · Germany
Tel: +49 551 999 500 · Fax: +49 551 999 50 111
E-Mail: customerservice@hogrefe.de

Hogrefe Publishing c/o Marston Book Services Ltd
160 Eastern Ave., Milton Park · Abingdon, OX14 4SB · UK
Tel: +44 1235 465577 · Fax +44 1235 465556
E-mail: direct.orders@marston.co.uk

HOGREFE

Order online at **www.hogrefe.com**
or call toll-free (800) 228-3749 (US only)